The Chair's Handbook

A guide for chairs of governing boards
of schools and academy trusts

8th edition
Emma Knights
National Governance Association
October 2020

Acknowledgments

We would like to thank all those members of the National Governance Association (NGA) who have informed our knowledge of the practice of governing boards over the years and of chairing up and down the country. We have also benefited from our growing number of Leading Governance partners who worked with us over the past seven years to provide governance leadership programmes.

Recognition should also go to Gillian Allcroft, NGA's former deputy chief executive, who co-authored the first six editions of this guide, and Judith Hicks, NGA's Head of Inspiring Governance, who contributed to the seventh edition. Thanks also to NGA staff, in particular Richard Crabb, Head of Communications, and Simon Richards, Chairs Development Manager, who have supported us in the production of this edition, and Sandra Solomon, who helps ensure this handbook reaches the reader.

Further comments and suggestions for improvement by our readers and members are always welcome to **emma.knights@nga.org.uk**.

Emma Knights
Chief Executive
National Governance Association

August 2020

Contents

Foreword

So, you've taken the plunge and stepped up to what I hope you will find is a most fascinating and important role – congratulations on taking up a position where you can really influence improvement for the children and young people in your school(s). This publication from the National Governance Association (NGA) should help you to navigate your way through the different aspects of the chair's role, supporting you to lead your board in governing the organisation well.

Whatever the size of your school or trust, you are now at the helm, with your headteacher or chief executive, of a complex organisation. It has never been more apparent, as structures evolve, that ethical and effective governance is crucial to ensuring that public funds are spent in a way that produces the very best outcomes for all our children. This handbook will point you to the best practice so that you can deliver real accountability for the provision in your school(s). The strategic role of the board enables the professionals in our schools to focus on delivering high-quality education, and you can now guide your board in setting the vision and the longer-term direction for the school(s).

Having been a chair of a number of governing boards over the years, I know the time, care, reflection and dedication the role takes. You are not on your own: NGA provides a family of chairs to share with and learn from. Our networks and Leading Governance development programmes provide clusters of peers, relationships which can sustain you. This handbook harnesses the expertise from many countries and many sectors, but also NGA's bespoke research about school governance in England. NGA's time to chair research over the past five years provides a substantive evidence base to draw from as well as the outcomes from our annual governance surveys.

The recent period of COVID-19 lockdown has made us introduce new ways of undertaking board business, moving to virtual meetings. While we can keep those elements of governing remotely which have made meetings more efficient, discussions more focused, and saved travel times at the end of the working day, we need to balance this with face-to-face interaction to build trusting relationships when visiting the school(s) you govern. Strategic discussions with senior leaders may well rightly go back to being in the same room, but perhaps with the opportunity for some who might otherwise have missed it to join remotely.

The national COVID-19 pandemic has highlighted a number of issues for schools, in particular as the hub for bringing together all those services that families and children rely on,

addressing disadvantage, and helping those in most need to catch up with their more affluent peers. And of course we must not forget the wellbeing of both our children and our staff which will be core to their learning recovery. These are issues I am sure your governing board will be discussing in the years to come.

It is your role to ensure that all the members of the board get to know your school or trust and understand how they can best make a difference. This handbook is only one of the many ways in which NGA can support you and your colleagues. The members' website has a plethora of resources in its Knowledge Centre and our experienced advice team is always at the end of the phone for our GOLD members when you need bespoke support in challenging times.

Our e-learning programme, NGA Learning Link, with its eight comprehensive core induction modules, part of a suite of fifty, can provide essential knowledge. When recruiting volunteers to the board you need to make sure you stress the expectations on induction, training and development.

Thank you for volunteering to take on what is likely be a challenging role – you will no doubt develop and learn, and I hope you enjoy this privilege to make the educational experience of the children and young people in your school(s) the very best that it can be.

Maggi Bull
Chair of the National Governance Association

National Governance Association

The National Governance Association (NGA) is the membership organisation for governors, trustees and clerks of state schools in England.

We are an independent, not-for-profit charity that aims to improve the educational standards and wellbeing of young people by increasing the effectiveness of governing boards and promoting high standards. We are expert leaders in school and trust governance, providing information, advice and guidance, professional development and e-learning.

We represent the views of governors, trustees and clerks at a national level and work closely with, and lobby, UK government and educational bodies.

Membership

NGA membership provides your school with access to a wealth of governance resources and tools. Whether it's through providing professional advice and guidance, practical resources and knowledge sharing or keeping you up to date on education news and policy, we can help you face new challenges as they arise.

GOLD governing board membership £275

- access independent and confidential advice through our GOLDline service
- copies of Governing Matters magazine to the home of every governor/trustee and a copy to the school
- a weekly e-newsletter featuring the latest education news and policy updates
- access to members-only content in our online Knowledge Centre
- complimentary copies of Welcome to Governance for all new governors and Welcome to Multi Academy Trusts for all new trustees
- a complimentary copy of The Chair's Handbook
- additional NGA guides available at a discounted rate
- three free places at NGA member conferences and events

Please check the NGA website for up-to-date membership details.

STANDARD governing board membership £97

- copies of Governing Matters magazine to the home of three governors/trustees and a copy to the school
- a weekly e-newsletter featuring the latest education news and policy updates
- access to members-only content in our online Knowledge Centre
- NGA guides available at a discounted rate
- a free place at NGA member conferences and events

Join us

For more information on joining, please get in touch.

0121 237 3780
www.nga.org.uk/membership

n|g|a| GOLDline
The NGA Advice Service

GOLDline is NGA's independent and confidential advice service available exclusively to GOLD governing board members.

Governing boards often face complex challenges. Our experts are available to deal with any questions you may have and the service is easily accessible online, by phone and email. Our advice covers strategic, procedural and legal information about governance.

Our advice service is supported by leading education law firm Browne Jacobson.

www.nga.org.uk/goldline

n g a National Governance Association
KNOWLEDGE CENTRE

The Knowledge Centre provides members with exclusive online access to best practice school governance guidance including finance; staffing; Ofsted; curriculum; special educational needs; legislation; and school improvement.

Practical governance resources include model policies; templates; checklists; information summaries; insights; case studies; and much more.

www.nga.org.uk/knowledge-centre

How to use this guide

This guide is about the responsibilities and the work of the chair of a governing body or of a board of trustees in state-funded schools in England. It should also be useful for vice chairs and those chairing committees. At certain points, where there is resonance with school governing, we quote from authors who have written on the role of the chair of boards in other sectors.

The language we use in this handbook

There are many different governance structures in the state school sector; this is a topic we cover in detail in other publications. However, the role of the chair of a board is extremely similar and the same principles of governance apply. To make the handbook easier to read we have taken the following approach.

We use the word 'schools' to include academies (including free schools). However, academy trust boards and academy committees are not covered by all the same regulations as maintained schools, and there may be some differences in relation to the precise procedures. The chair of an academy may need to check their trust's funding agreement, articles of association and any schemes of delegation to be certain whether a particular provision applies equally to them (we refer to these three documents as academy documentation). There are, however, few significant differences in practice between chairing a board of trustees and a maintained school. Where those do occur we highlight the difference.

We use the phrase 'governing board' to cover both the maintained governing body and the academy board of trustees, and only differentiate between the two where we are referring to one but not the other. Some readers will be chairing a committee of the main board, but much of the content will apply.

We use the phrase 'academy committee' if we need to distinguish those governing at academy level within a multi academy trust (MAT). There are a variety of names for these committees; many MATs use the term local governing bodies (LGBs), but this suggests an autonomy and an equivalence with maintained school governing bodies, which is not the case.

We use the word 'governor' as shorthand to mean those governing: governors, trustees and members of academy committees. It is essential that a chair knows whether s/he is chairing a board of trustees, governors or an academy committee within a MAT. Trustees do have different legal responsibilities and these are covered fully in our induction guide Welcome to a Multi Academy Trust.

We use 'headteacher' to describe the lead executive as most chairs of governing boards are still working with a headteacher. However, in a federation, the lead executive being held to account is likely to be an executive principal, while in a MAT, it is likely to be a chief executive held to account by a MAT board of trustees. There will also usually be academy-level committees of the main board where headteachers work with those committee chairs.

We use the term 'future chair' to denote any governor or trustee who is likely to take the position of chair of the governing board in the near future as part of a succession plan.

. . . .

The handbook does not cover the role of chair of an interim executive board (IEB), which is nearly always put in place in schools where both governance and operational leadership are weak. As its name indicates, an IEB is more than the non-executive role of other governors and trustees; it is more 'hands-on' than governance in other school settings and very likely to take up more time. Moreover, it should be a paid role. Many of the principles and practice of chairing will still apply.

Leading governance in schools

1

Good governance is vital to any successful organisation fulfilling its purpose. In the state-funded sector, there is the added task of ensuring that public money is used well. Governing boards are central to the effective accountability of schools and ensuring children and young people reach their potential.

> ❝ Governance determines who has the power, who makes the decisions, how other players make their voice heard, and how account is rendered. ❞

Institute on Governance, Canada

Governing more than one school

A governing body of a maintained federation or a board of trustees of a multi academy trust (MAT) is responsible for more than one school. Although this does not materially affect the nature of the role of the chair, it could present different practical challenges in terms of setting the priorities for each school in the group, understanding the performance of each school and holding the professional leadership to account.

If you are the chair of the governing body of an academy within a MAT, you are in fact chairing a committee of the board of trustees. The academy-level governance within a MAT is often called a local governing body (LGB), but it does not have the same responsibility as a maintained school governing body. The chair of the MAT board must ensure that the chairs at academy level understand what duties and responsibilities have been delegated to the academy committees by the board of trustees.

Indeed, it is imperative that all who govern within the structure understand which decisions are made at each level. These vary from MAT to MAT and will be set out in the MAT's scheme of delegation (SoD). This understanding has proved to be a problem in some MATs, and there are now a number of resources specifically designed to help those involved in governance of MATs, which are covered in our guide Welcome to a Multi Academy Trust.

Governing more than one school may also affect some of the ways the business is conducted, and we will refer to any substantial variations where they exist. There may be particular differences in the appointment process and role of a chair of an academy committee in a MAT. It is also almost always the case that the performance management of the headteacher will be the responsibility of a senior executive within the trust, although s/he is likely to involve the chair in the appraisal process.

There are now many other partnerships in which schools can engage. However, the governance of those partnerships will not be the same as the governance of a federation or MAT, where the governing board has direct responsibility for the performance of a number of schools. Governing boards should ensure they are happy with the proposed governance arrangement of any partnership the school(s) is entering.

1.1 Core functions of school or trust governing boards

Governing boards in all types of school have four core functions:

1. Ensuring clarity of vision, ethos and strategic direction
2. Holding the executive leaders to account for the educational performance of the school and its pupils, and the performance management of staff
3. Overseeing the financial performance of the organisation and making sure its money is well spent
4. Ensuring the voices of stakeholders are heard

A spotlight on school governance

In the past, governance was a rather overlooked component of school leadership. The education profession does not always appreciate the power of accountability through governance in the same way that it does through inspection and 'performance tables', and school leaders may not have had the experience of seeing great governance in practice. But given that more decisions have been devolved to school or group level, particularly but not only in academy trusts, the importance of governance is now more widely acknowledged in ensuring that schools in England thrive and provide a good standard of education to pupils.

Ofsted's 2018/19 annual report found that 86% of all schools were judged 'good' or 'outstanding' for 'overall effectiveness' at their most recent inspection, (87% of primary schools, 76% of secondary schools and 92% of special schools were rated as good or outstanding), which still leaves 14% of schools judged 'requires improvement' or 'inadequate' at that last inspection. We have since had a new inspection framework and we return to the issue of Ofsted inspections in chapter 5.5.

This increased focus on school governance has brought greater acknowledgment of the position of chair by policy-makers. For the past six years the Department for Education (DfE) has been subsidising development programmes for chairs and clerks to governing boards and designating national leaders of governance (NLGs) to support chairs (see chapter 8). NGA has provided these programmes through our Leading Governance partnership for chairs, future chairs and also for boards of MATs and federations. Both these programmes are fully funded by the DfE (at least until March 2021) and therefore free to eligible schools. To find out more, please visit www.nga.org.uk/leadinggovernance.

1.2 Ethical governance

It is imperative that those who govern have high ethical standards, which correspond not only to the values of the organisation but also to the seven Nolan principles agreed by the Committee for Standards in Public Life:

- **Selflessness:** should act solely in terms of the public interest. They should not do so in order to gain financial or other benefits for themselves, their family or their friends.
- **Integrity:** should not place themselves under any financial or other obligation to outside individuals or organisations that might seek to influence them in the performance of their official duties.
- **Objectivity:** should make choices on merit.
- **Accountability:** are accountable for their decisions and actions to the public, and must submit themselves to whatever scrutiny is appropriate to their office.

- **Openness:** should be as open as possible about all the decisions and actions that they take. They should give reasons for their decisions and restrict information only when the wider public interest clearly demands it.
- **Honesty:** have a duty to declare any private interests relating to their public duties and to take steps to resolve any conflicts arising in a way that protects the public interest.
- **Leadership:** should promote and support these principles by leadership and example.

NGA was part of a commission that in January 2019 published the Framework for Ethical Leadership in Education, which defines a set of virtues, building on the Nolan principles, against which both executive and non-executive leaders can test their decision-making in educational leadership. It is helpful if the standards to which we expect to be held, or hold others, are explicit. As role models for the young, how we behave as leaders is as important as what we do. Leadership is shown through the following personal characteristics or virtues:

- **Trust:** leaders should be trustworthy and reliable. They hold trust on behalf of children and should be beyond reproach. We are honest about our motivations.
- **Wisdom:** leaders should use experience, knowledge, insight, understanding and good sense to make sound judgments. They should demonstrate restraint and self-awareness, act calmly and rationally, exercising moderation and propriety as they serve their schools and colleges wisely.
- **Kindness:** leaders demonstrate respect, generosity of spirit, understanding and good temper. Where unavoidable conflict occurs, difficult messages should be given humanely.
- **Justice:** leaders should work fairly, for the good of children from all backgrounds. They should seek to enable all young people to lead useful, happy and fulfilling lives.
- **Service:** leaders should be conscientious and dutiful. We should demonstrate humility and self-control, supporting the structures and rules that safeguard quality. Our actions should protect high-quality education.
- **Courage:** leaders should work courageously in the best interests of children and young people. We protect their safety and their right to a broad, effective and creative education. We should hold one another to account courageously.
- **Optimism:** leaders should be positive and encouraging. Despite difficulties and pressures, we are developing excellent education to change the world for the better.

The not-for-profit literature talks about duties of the trustees that have their basis in law:

- duty of care
- duty of loyalty
- duty of obedience

These largely relate to the fiduciary aspects of the governing board's work. Given the context for schools in England we suggest that two others would emphasise the full range of responsibility:

- duty of courage
- duty of imagination

These principles, virtues and duties need to be demonstrated in the behaviour of board members, both in meetings and elsewhere, and visible within a code of conduct (see chapter 3.2), which can help in setting the expectations and then holding each other to them.

 No crooks; no cronies; no cowards.

Chair of Aviva quoted in the Tyson Report on the Recruitment and Development of Non-Executive Directors

Conflicts of interest

School and trust governing boards have not always taken potential conflicts of interest seriously, and in the past have often failed to question or exclude those with conflicts of interest in case that was interpreted as mistrust. Furthermore, consideration was in practice often limited to financial gain, rather than the very common interests of family and friends.

A declaration of interest should include any links with individuals, businesses, contractors, directorships or shareholdings in an organisation from which the school may purchase goods or services. Governors and trustees should also declare where there is a relationship with someone who is directly employed by the school or trust. They should include interests of related persons such as a parent, spouse, cohabitee, child or business partner where influence could be exerted by that person over a governor or trustee. Governors whose children attend the school may need to declare an interest where the outcome of a decision could directly affect them or their child, for example, changes to the before- and after-school provision that the parent currently uses. Those governors paid to work in the school should not be involved in panels considering exclusions or staff grievances, as it is highly likely they will have prior knowledge of the individual and consequently there would be a reasonable doubt about whether they could act impartially.

The Education Skills Funding Agency (ESFA) has in recent years tightened the rules regarding related party transactions: any payment over £20,000 made to a related party has to be approved in advance by the ESFA and all have to be reported to the ESFA. Chairs who govern in academies should ensure they fully understand the rules set out in the ESFA's Academies Financial Handbook (the most recent edition came into effect on 1 September 2020).

NGA suggests that wherever possible financial conflicts and indeed other types of conflicts should be avoided, rather than just declared, as perceptions are important and acting on declarations has been patchy. Indeed, some boards act as though the declaring of an interest is sufficient, and no proper consideration is actually given as to whether the conflict is too large to remain governing (for example, being married to a senior leader at the school/trust) or whether they need to withdraw from the discussion. It is very common for individuals to struggle to see how their other interests might affect their ability to act entirely in the interest of the organisation being governed. Where a conflict of interest exists on a given issue, the chair must ensure that the relevant governor or trustee must absent themselves from further discussion and voting on that matter. In some very serious but uncommon cases, removal from the meeting may not be sufficient to remove the influence from the discussion.

1.3 Effective governance

NGA has identified eight elements that research and practice tell us are essential for good governance. These apply to whatever type of school you govern. These eight elements are needed to transform the team of diverse people with a range of skills, experience and knowledge into a highly effective governing board.

Eight elements of effective governance	
1	the right people around the table
2	understanding the role and responsibilities
3	good chairing
4	professional clerking
5	good relationships based on trust
6	knowing the school or trust– the data, the staff, the parents, the children, the community
7	committed to asking challenging questions
8	confident to have courageous conversations in the interests of the children and young people

Without all eight elements in place, it is unlikely that a governing board will be able to play its part to the full. NGA suggests that good chairing is the most important element, as a good chair will ensure that the other seven elements are in place. That may be a daunting ask, but anyone volunteering to take on this role needs to understand the depth of the responsibility – one that relies on personal attributes and the support of the rest of the governing board to be successful.

We will return to reviewing effectiveness in chapter 3.5.

1.4 Accountable governance

Governing boards are part of the school accountability system. There is upward accountability that is recognised in the law: the governing board of a maintained school or federation is answerable for its performance and conduct to the local authority, the board of academy trustees to the secretary of state for education, and academy committees within a MAT to the board of the trustees.

The board is also accountable in the broader sense to the community, taxpayers, parents and pupils. The chair needs to ensure the board takes this responsibility seriously in the way it carries out its decision-making and reporting of those decisions. NGA believes that some boards have not been taking this aspect of their role seriously, despite the clear requirement to do so.

In an academy trust, the board of trustees is also accountable to the trust members, who have a limited but distinct role as guardians of governance. NGA has produced guidance on the role of members: www.nga.org.uk/MAT-role-of-members.

1.5 The role of the chair

The chair leads the governing board, with the support from the vice chair, ensuring it fulfils its functions well. The culture of the board is largely determined by its chair, for better or worse. A good chair will ensure its focus is on the strategic, and it is no exaggeration to say that the success or failure of a governing board depends heavily on the calibre of its chair.

  " It is only when you become aware of the range, scope and incredible responsibility of the job that you realise there is an almost limitless opportunity to be ineffective, unless you are totally clear about how you are going to set about it. "

Sir John Harvey-Jones

The role of the chair is not described in legislation. The chair is first among equals but has no defined individual power. The governing body or board of trustees is a corporate entity; the power and authority rests with the governing board as a whole. The chair may need to take chair's action (see chapter 6.6) in an emergency, but any such action must be reported to the whole governing board as soon as possible.

A good chair works well with school leaders to advise and shape proposals to be discussed at the board meetings. In effect, the chair runs the board and the headteacher runs the school, but their relationship is key to ensuring the governing board and senior leadership team establish a vision and strategic priorities for the school(s). The chair's ability to build good, productive relationships with a range of different people is absolutely critical.

The chair should facilitate the governing board working as a team to challenge, support and contribute to the strategic leadership of the school. As well as a leader, the chair is at times a confidant, a manager, a critical friend, a sounding board, a catalyst, a cheerleader, an ambassador, an arbitrator, a negotiator, a networker and possibly a mentor or coach. The balance of these roles adopted by any chair will depend on the situation at hand, in particular the experience and strengths of the headteacher.

However, even this list can underplay the role a good chair plays in encouraging the headteacher to develop proposals that are fit for purpose, and ensuring that the governing board is active in driving the strategic direction of the school. S/he is likely to visit the school more often than others on the board, in particular to meet the head, and thus will have a greater understanding of the progress of the school.

The chair will usually have more involvement than other governors in particular tasks such as complaints. But almost all of these are not formally restricted to the chair, and it is important that tasks are not assumed to belong to the chair. Sharing them among the board and, where appropriate, delegating them to school leaders leads to a more sustainable role and a stronger board.

We have created a role description of the chair (opposite) that can be used by a new chair or a headteacher, or when reviewing the chair's performance. When selecting a new chair or developing successors, this needs to be considered alongside the full range of qualities needed by a good chair (see chapter 2.1).

Appointing the chair

In maintained schools and standalone academies this is a decision for the governing board. NGA members can see NGA's recommended process for this in the guidance centre at www.nga.org.uk/Knowledge-Centre.

In MATs the chair of the board of trustees is appointed by the other trustees. The chair of any academy committee (usually called local governing bodies) will be appointed according to the rules that the MAT board has put in place. This may affect the role of the committee chair, as the MAT may retain at trustee board level some of the functions described above.

Those appointing the chair should consider the skills and attributes needed and whether the candidate possesses those. See chapter 2 for further information on the required competencies. NGA members can download a pdf version of the document (which also contains the role specification covered in chapter 2) at www.nga.org.uk/Knowledge-Centre.

Learning from other sectors

The role of the chair of governors should be viewed in the same light as that of the chair of the board in any other sector – whether private, public or third – and this guide draws from those other sources. For example, the literature from the private sector shows that the role of the chair is a demanding, complex, multifaceted and high-profile responsibility requiring a broad set of capabilities of a very high order. These include the ability to resolve disputes; to minimise dysfunctional interactions; to enable the board to reach a consensus; to network; to establish positive relationships with local political figures; to be able to 'take the flak' during critical incidents; to have credibility with the professional workforce; to think strategically; and to solve problems.

Professor Chris James, professor of educational leadership and management at the University of Bath, et al have emphasised the importance of the values and motivations that underpin a board chair's approach to and practice in the role. They suggest the behaviours of ineffective board chairs can provide food for thought: "Being overly eager to please others; lacking a strong mind of their own; always insisting that their view is the correct one; and paying too much attention to detail and neglecting the 'bigger picture'."

On the other hand, the characteristics of outstanding board chairs include: "Flexibility in the operation of board processes; having an open style of leadership; and preparing themselves for their role… a high level of integrity; … high ethical standards in respect of their own behaviour; and demonstrating empathy."

Research in 2009 concluded, from surveys undertaken internationally in both private and public sectors, that success at board level does relate to the chair's performance. In particular to the chair:

- working well with other board members to achieve organisational goals
- taking a long-term view
- having an understanding of the cultural context of the organisation – what works in one organisation may not work in another
- having a considered approach to risk
- balancing hard and soft skills – on the one hand being robust and strong in the role, and on the other being able to raise sensitive issues and encouraging an open debate
- following through on governance initiatives
- acknowledging skill or experience gaps on the current board and addressing these

In his 2014 report into the governance of the Co-operative Group, Lord Myners noted that to be effective a chair needs to play a broad role incorporating the following elements:

- being a source of wise counsel to the CEO, providing credible advice based on years of experience while respecting executive responsibility
- creating the right board environment for high-quality debate and decision-making
- managing dynamics so that contentious or 'difficult' issues are raised and addressed
- challenging and holding executives to account as needed
- upholding the highest standards of corporate governance
- interfacing effectively with a range of external and internal stakeholders

There is also much guidance and literature from the third sector, which is perhaps most applicable given the similarity of the legal framework, particularly for academies. We have integrated learning and experiences from across the charity sector in the UK, and where relevant we also include international learning in this Handbook.

A literature review the Association of Chairs commissioned about the effectiveness of chairs of not-for-profit organisations found that charity chairs who are perceived to be effective with high impact display similar characteristics to good chairs of for-profit and public organisations. Good interpersonal and leadership skills distinguished effective from ineffective chairs, while being authoritarian and following a personal agenda are two key characteristics of a poor chair. The five broad personal qualities that were found to identify exceptional chairs are: motivation and style;

Role description for the chair of the board

The role of the chair of a governing board in a state-funded school or academy trust in England is comparable to that of the chair of the board in any other sector. The governing board works as a team to challenge, support and contribute to the strategic leadership of the school. Although the chair has no defined individual power, s/he should have significant influence on the board's culture and conduct. A good chair works well with school leaders to advise and shape proposals to be discussed at the board meetings, ensuring the focus is strategic.

Role purpose

To provide leadership to the governing board and ensure that governors/trustees fulfil their functions for the proper governance of the school(s).

Leading governance in schools

- ensure the governing board sets a clear vision and strategy for the school(s)
- ensure that the governing board and headteacher have a shared vision and sense of purpose
- lead the board in monitoring the headteacher's implementation of the school strategy
- set the culture of the governing board, balancing and valuing both the support and challenge responsibilities
- carry out a performance review of each board member (or delegate this to the vice chair)
- ensure the board acts as a team
- ensure that there is a plan for succession for the chair, vice chair and any committee chairs
- recommend limits on office to ensure there is always a mix of new and experienced members

Leading and developing the team

- ensure the board has the required skills and commitment to govern well, and that appointments made fill any identified skills gaps and ensure a diverse team
- ensure all members of the board have a thorough understanding of their role and receive appropriate induction and training as required
- ensure that board members are involved and feel valued
- encourage their development
- ensure members of the board act reasonably and in line with the board's agreed code of conduct
- develop a good working relationship with the vice chair, ensuring s/he is kept fully informed and delegating tasks as appropriate

The chair, the headteacher and accountability

- build a professional relationship with the headteacher that allows for honest conversations, acting as a sounding board and ensuring there are no surprises at meetings
- to meet regularly (normally monthly) with the headteacher
- ensure that there are transparent and effective processes for the recruitment and induction of the headteacher
- ensure appropriate governor/trustee involvement in the recruitment of senior leaders
- ensure all board members concentrate on their strategic role and hold the headteacher to account
- ensure all board members receive information that allows them to fulfil their function
- oversee and participate in the headteacher's performance review, ensuring that appropriate continuing professional development (CPD) is provided
- ensure that the headteacher provides staff with an understanding of the role of the governing board and acts as link between the two
- where required, represent the governing board in its dealings with external partners and be an advocate for the school/trust
- attend school functions (plays/sports days/prize-giving) as appropriate and encourage other governors to do so
- ensure that complaints made to the governing board are dealt with in a timely and effective manner
- play a lead role in any decision to suspend the headteacher

NGA members can download a pdf version of the role description of the document at www.nga.org.uk/Knowledge-Centre.

Leading school improvement

- ensure the board is involved at a strategic level in the school's self-evaluation process and that this feeds into its key priorities
- ensure the board's business is focused on the strategic priorities
- take the lead in representing the governing board at relevant external meetings with agencies such as Ofsted, the DfE and the local authority
- ensure the board has the information it needs to monitor the progress of pupils and consider appropriate actions to improve outcomes
- to ensure the board has good knowledge of the school(s) and has mechanisms in place to obtain and listen to the views of parents, pupils and staff

Leading governing board business

- work with the clerk and the headteacher to plan for board meetings, ensuring that agendas focus on the board's key responsibilities and strategic priorities and reduce unnecessary paperwork
- chair meetings effectively and promote an open culture on the governing board that allows ideas and discussion to thrive while ensuring clear decisions are reached as quickly as possible
- collaborate with the clerk to establish effective working procedures and sound committee structures
- ensure that decisions taken at the meetings of the governing body are implemented
- to ensure the governing board appoints a professional clerk capable of providing advice on the board's functions and that s/he is appraised and developed

capacity to lead; personal attributes; ability to relate; and ability to advance the organisation externally. These were the polar opposites of less-effective chairs.

The high-profile demise of Kids Company in 2015 highlighted the challenges of the trustee board, especially when working with a charismatic chief executive. After its inquiry, the House of Commons' Public Administration and Constitutional Affairs Committee concluded: "The Charity Commission's guidance to Trustees warns that Trustees should not allow their judgment to be swayed by personal prejudices or dominant personalities, but this is what occurred in Kids Company. This resulted in Trustees suspending their usual critical faculties… The length of the Chief Executive and Chair's tenures were not conducive to challenging the Chief Executive herself. There was a clear link between the failure to correct serious weaknesses in the organisation, and the failure to refresh its leadership."

Despite this long service, the chair did not fully appreciate the role for which he and his fellow trustees had volunteered: "The evidence Mr Yentob gave to the Committee suggests a lack of proper attention to his duties as Chair of Trustees and a continuing inability to recognise those failures. With his fellow Trustees he was unwilling or unable to impose sufficient control. Together, they failed to exercise their proper function as Trustees."

1.6 A leadership position

The board provides leadership to the organisation, and its work should be thought of as a corporate activity, a collective endeavour. A good board comprises a group of leaders committed to a common cause; whereas a collection of powerful personalities each seeking advantage or pursuing a particular interest of their own is a weak board. The chair needs to ensure the team operates in that first mode, not the second.

Being the chair of a governing board is not only a critical position required to ensure effective governance, it is also a trust/school leadership role. This was first fully recognised in 2011 by the then National College of School Leadership bringing school governance within its remit with the first edition of Leading Governance, published jointly with NGA. Ofsted also acknowledged the role of the board in 2012 when it first included governance as part of its leadership and management judgment when inspecting schools.

The style of leadership the chair adopts should flow from the school's values and ethos, although this will vary with individuals. However, absolutely central to the role is the ability to build trust through consistent ethical behaviour and good judgment. Good communication and negotiation are key. Trust can take time to build but can be lost in a moment of thoughtlessness or recklessness.

Behaviours that will help a chair build trust include: listening to other opinions and ideas; role-modelling behaviour that is respectful; conducting oneself in a professional manner; meeting commitments and deadlines; and keeping the relevant people informed via professional communications.

The board's decision-making needs to be rational and free of vested interests, but this may be approached in various ways by its individual members, with weight being given to different issues or types of evidence. The chair has to enforce objectivity in every discussion, while respecting different experiences and ensuring the organisation's values and mission are upheld. However, chairing a board involves much more than tending to the rational and dispassionate dispatch of business. It is also about recognising the board as a social group with group dynamics that can affect its ability to function well.

There is therefore a significant element of talent management within the role, developing the individuals' talents as well as their ability to function well as a team. Equally, the board should not lose sight of its role in the talent management of the paid leadership team.

The chair will need to be a confident advocate for the school and the board's chosen strategy outside board meetings. S/he also needs to ensure that all relevant parties (often termed stakeholders) – pupils, parents, staff, the wider community – have been able to make their voices heard.

In chapter 2 we consider the skills expected of someone taking the chair, but these can be summarised as intellectual intelligence, emotional intelligence and ethical intelligence.

1.7 Ensuring a strategic focus

The chair must ensure that the governing board first defines the vision, ethos and strategic direction of the school and then concentrates on monitoring whether the school is on course to meet its goals, rather than interfering in the headteacher's role. The school strategy should drive the business of the governing board for the year. An effective school strategy document will describe not only where the school/trust wants to be, but how it will know if it is progressing in the right direction. In September 2020, NGA published the second edition of Being Strategic: a guide for governing boards in partnership with the Association of School and College Leaders and the National Association of Head Teachers, which has more guidance on how to achieve this. A chair should ask the clerk to provide all the members of the board with a copy.

It might be expected that a headteacher will annually propose a draft strategy to the governing board with priorities for the coming year after carrying out an evaluation of where the school wants to be. However, not all headteachers are familiar with the discipline of the strategic planning cycle, nor have experience of drafting concise documents fit for prompting discussion of future challenges and strategy. The chair may therefore initially need to be quite heavily involved – and also possibly the vice chair and committee chairs – in helping to shape the draft being proposed by the headteacher for a decision by the governing board. This is especially likely with a first-time headteacher.

An annual strategy review session with the senior leadership team is essential. This session needs to be outside a usual governing board meeting, without the constraints of the usual agenda, and one in which all ideas can be suggested, and all participants engage. The process may also involve consultation with pupils and parents as well as staff. A chair at academy level within a MAT will need to consider their committee's role and how that fits within the MAT-wide strategy-setting process.

Governance needs to be generative as well as strategic. Generative thinking needs to precede the strategy-setting and problem-solving: it is thinking and discussion that searches for opportunities and generates ideas, some of which provide solutions. It is powerful and should shape much of what happens in an organisation. A good chair should ensure this happens by providing the opportunity and the culture to reflect and debate.

Individuals who routinely think generatively are often seen as insightful or creative. When teams attempt to engage in this way it is often labelled 'brainstorming' or 'thinking outside the box', and governing boards need to be able to engage with senior leaders in this way. This generative mode of governance requires the interplay of ideas, with participants actively listening to each other, all contributing and building on each other's suggestions. It thrives on dialogue and deliberations among participants with different perspectives.

This way of working may not be familiar to all the board and a chair might need to encourage some more reserved or less experienced members to participate. The more hypotheses and angles of vision, the more likely it is that perceptive insights will materialise and issues coming over the horizon will be identified. When the board is in generative mode, as opposed to monitoring mode, in a meeting with a more formal agenda, the chair should adopt a slightly different approach to managing the time and should not restrict the scope unduly. A comment that at first appears out of the ordinary might end up sparking a useful discussion.

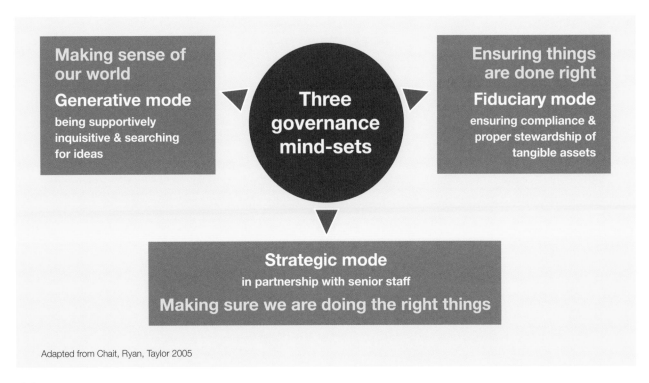

Making sense of our world

Generative mode

being supportively inquisitive & searching for ideas

Three governance mind-sets

Ensuring things are done right

Fiduciary mode

ensuring compliance & proper stewardship of tangible assets

Strategic mode

in partnership with senior staff

Making sure we are doing the right things

Adapted from Chait, Ryan, Taylor 2005

> " Trustees are typically situated at the edge of the organisation, close enough to understand the organisation's aims, operations and cultures, yet far enough removed to have some perspective, distance and detachment. Board members usually embrace the institution's mission but have little at risk personally or professionally. From this vantage point, trustees can see the larger picture, overall patterns and tell-tale anomalies. "

Governance as Leadership by Chait, Ryan & Taylor

The chair should ensure the governing board is able to deal with problems and related proposals professionally – both in terms of the skills on the board, and the way in which it conducts its business. There must be rigorous application of objective analysis, followed by sound judgment based on ethics and the school's values. At the same time a chair cannot ignore that instinct and emotions may well play a part in decision-making and learn to manage those situations so that the best decisions are made.

The board has legal and compliance duties it must fulfil. These are important responsibilities, but for some boards these can monopolise its time so that it concentrates on procedures, rather than the school's mission to provide a good education to its pupils. This is most likely to occur with trustees and governors who come from outside education and are in their professional comfort zones with organisational management. The chair needs to be alert to this and encourage all to contribute to the generative and strategic work as well as the fiduciary. The board needs

to be adding value to the work of the trust/school and not just obeying a set of rules and regulations. It is not there to provide pro-bono advice to supplement the work of school leaders and trust executives.

Some boards do get distracted at times by the urgency of current events and the excitement of intervention, but that is likely to be the province of the executive. Ofsted has identified some schools that were distracted from pupil attainment when undertaking structural change, which involved significant time of both senior leaders and the governing board.

If practices have been adopted in the past that are not truly strategic and are taking time away from the governing board carrying out its functions as the accountable body, these need to be discussed at a meeting and future arrangements agreed. For example, an issue that commonly needs review is the involvement of governors at too early a stage in staffing issues (see chapter 2.4). The way in which the chair (with the clerk's support) oversees the agenda for meetings is another key tool in ensuring the governing board concentrates on strategic matters, while not overlooking its fiduciary responsibilities (see chapter 6.3).

Once the governing board has set the strategic priorities for the year, it leaves the headteacher or chief executive to devise the plan for achieving these and to lead the staff team in implementing the plan. The governing board's role is then to monitor, and the chair must ensure the governing board stays within its remit and does not step into the management of the school/trust.

Strategy development

A visual representation is provided by Caroline Copeman (2014) after David Fishel's 2003 book Boards That Work: a guide for charity trustees, which may help boards and senior staff to establish the right balance of responsibilities. The balance of the monitoring will change slightly over time depending on the health of the organisation, as well as the experience of the headteacher and the board, and the size of the organisation.

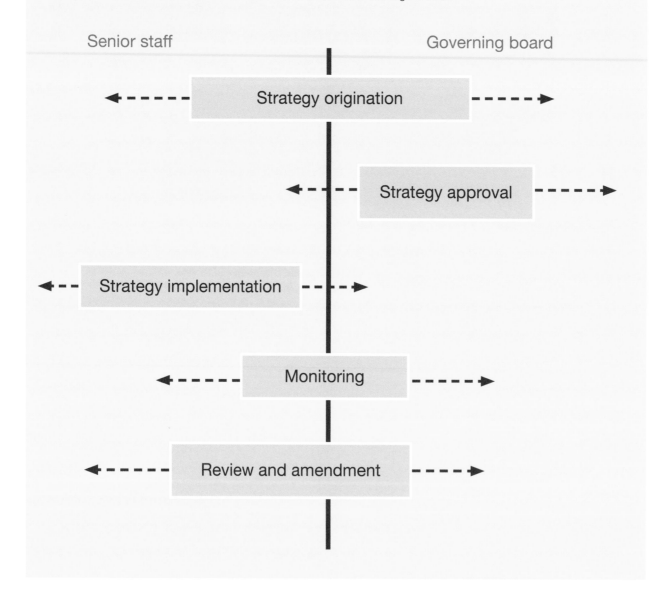

Strategic

Where are we now, where do we want to be (the vision) and how will we get there?

This involves setting the values, ethos and direction of the school with targets for long- and medium-term strategic priorities; providing oversight and monitoring of performance and setting the culture for performance management and development; assessing risks; agreeing on a budget to support the priorities and taking major spending decisions; agreeing only the principles and strategic direction of policies.

Operational

Delivery of the agreed strategy.

This is day-to-day management; short-term planning and monitoring; spending within agreed budget headings; recruitment and deployment of staff below the leadership team; supporting the improvement of teaching and learning; ensuring the performance management and CPD of staff; discipline in relation to individual staff or children; developing and implementing policies and procedures to deliver the vision.

1.8 Culture

❝ The board should foster a common culture, values and ethos across the whole organisation, ensuring it is reflected consistently in both its policies and its practices. ❞

DfE Governance Handbook

The culture of an organisation – the way things get done around here – should flow from its values and ethos. It may have developed over many years and might not be perceived in the same way by everyone. The culture will usually be affected by a change of senior leadership, but if it truly comes from the school's values and ethos, it should stand the test of time.

The board should set and safeguard an ethos of high expectations of everyone in the school community. This includes high expectations for the behaviour, progress and attainment of all pupils, and for the conduct and professionalism of both staff and the board themselves.

❝ A strategy that is at odds with a company's culture is doomed. Culture trumps strategy every time – culture eats strategy for breakfast. ❞

Attributed to Peter Drucker and popularised in 2006 by Mark Fields, president of Ford Motor Company

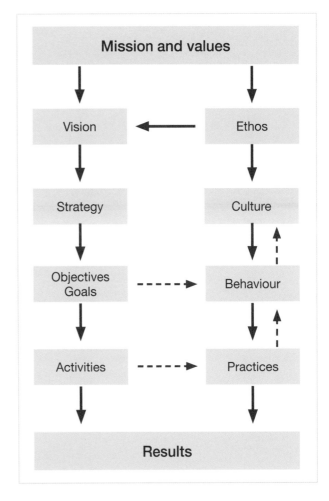

This much-quoted axiom does not render strategies redundant but emphasises the need for a culture that supports the strategy, and vice versa.

Much of NGA's day-to-day work answering queries from GOLD members concerns getting structure and process correct – the compliance aspect of the board's functions. However, although a structure can get in the way or conversely be a positive influence, structures and processes on their own never guarantee performance. It is the people and their behaviours that deliver the results envisioned in the strategy, and the culture that enables them to do so, or, conversely, inhibits them from doing so.

The chair needs to make sure the governing board is aware of the culture and climate – the way things feel – at the school, and to do that must make sure they hear from the school's staff. This has often been overlooked by governing boards not wanting to confuse the lines of management; however, it is becoming increasingly important as staff workload and retention become more of an issue. As the

secretary of state for education said at NGA's 2018 summer conference: "Fundamentally this is a people business. There is nothing more important in education than the people delivering it. Great teachers, great heads – and of course great governors." It is imperative that boards understand staff morale and consider what needs to be done to ensure the culture is aligned with their vision and strategy, not acting against it (see chapter 5.2).

All schools should embrace the value of being a learning organisation at every level, but how this materialises may vary and should be the concern of the board. The chair has a role in maintaining a healthy culture by championing professional development at all levels, from the board to non-teaching staff, and ensuring that the board is aware of workload implications on staff before making decisions.

Much of leadership concerns managing change, and although the board will set the direction, it is the school senior leaders who will manage the change with staff and other stakeholders on a day-to-day basis. However, there will be times when the chair is needed to facilitate or support this. Change of any type can be difficult to embed, but if cultural change is required this will be a significant challenge for which all parties need to prepare. One example of cultural change occurs when a school joins a MAT; even if the values and ethos of the MAT mirror those of the school, the change to becoming part of a larger organisation and losing the school's autonomy is significant. The governing board of the individual school being replaced by a committee of the board of trustees is a fundamental change that both the chair of the previous board and the chair of the new committee need to lead. We return to this in chapter 5.6.

 Tips on leading governance

Be familiar with:

- the structure within which you chair: a single academy trust, a MAT, a maintained school or federation
- the four core functions of governing boards of schools and trusts
- good governance is ethical, effective and accountable
- the Framework for Ethical Leadership in Education
- the eight elements of effective governance
- the three modes of governance: generative, strategic and fiduciary
- and balance the five aspects of the chair's role:

1. Leading and developing the team: chapter 3
2. The relationship with the headteacher/chief executive: chapter 4
3. Leading school improvement: see chapter 5
4. Leading governing board business: see chapter 6
5. Ensuring a succession plan: see chapter 7

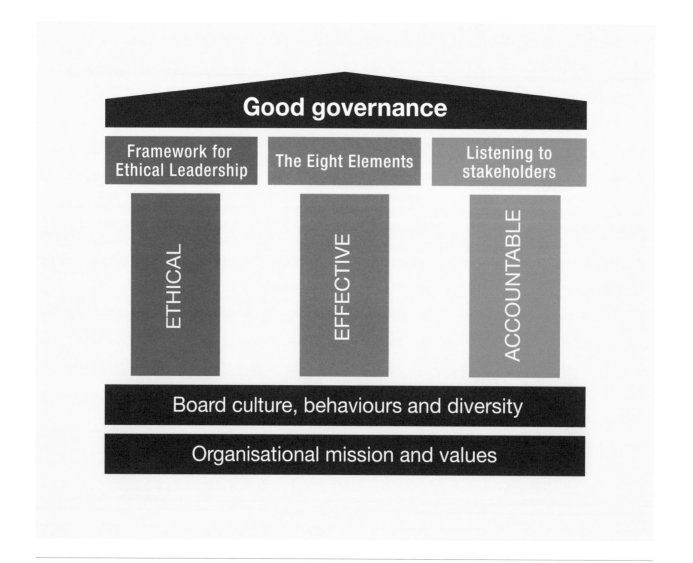

Becoming the chair

A good chair is essential to good governance. Anyone who is considering putting themselves forward or nominating someone else to lead the board needs to consider the commitment, time, skills, knowledge and especially the personal attributes required.

The governing body of a maintained school must elect a chair and vice chair from among their number, and this must be done at a meeting of the full governing body, except in extremely rare circumstances when the secretary of state may use her/his power to nominate as chair an additional governor whom s/he has appointed. Whenever a vacancy arises for the chair (see chapter 7), the governing body must elect a new chair at the next governing body meeting. The vice chair may only stand in for the chair on a temporary basis.

In academy trusts, the articles of association will state how the chair is appointed. This is often by election but it can also include appointment, particularly in the case of academy committees (often termed local governing bodies)

of multi academy trusts (MATs). Where local academy chairs are appointed by the trust board or executive, this is sometimes taken advantage of to put someone in place who will be compliant. However, this undermines good governance (see chapter 1).

Term of office

In standalone academies (sometimes termed single academy trusts), the articles usually require that the board of trustees must elect the chair annually at the first meeting of the year.

In maintained schools, before electing the chair, the governing body decides the period of office until a fresh election is held. NGA recommends that the period should not significantly exceed one year, as this allows an opportunity to reflect on the office-holder's performance and gives the chair the opportunity to restate her/his willingness to continue or to stand down.

NGA recommends that no one serves as chair in one school or trust for more than six consecutive years. This six-year period is recommended as a maximum, not as an optimum period of office, and there may be very good reasons not to accept renomination after a shorter period. There will of course be times when continuity is seen as important, but these occasions should very much be the exception. One example is when a new head has been appointed, but even then a new chair could be appropriate. Another could be the school joining or forming a federation or a MAT; this will entirely depend on the particular circumstances. In some cases it will a good opportunity for a fresh start, whereas in others it might necessitate a period of stability with a known chair.

DfE competencies for a chair: Part 1

- understands the importance of their non-executive leadership role, not just in their current position but in terms of their contribution to improving education locally or regionally
- sets high expectations for conduct and behaviour for all those in governance and is an exemplary role model in demonstrating these
- leads by example to avoid, declare and manage conflicts of interest
- thinks strategically about the future direction of the organisation and steps needed to achieve goals
- leads the board and executive leaders in ensuring operational decisions contribute to strategic priorities
- provides effective leadership of organisational change, even when this is difficult
- understands different leadership styles and applies these appropriately to enhance their personal effectiveness

Who cannot be the chair?

The headteacher may not stand or be elected to be chair, nor may any other employee at the school (in either a maintained school or an academy). Associate members are also excluded from taking the chair as they are not governors (this also applies to individuals appointed to committees in academies).

2.1 The role requirements

Candidates for the role of chair should be able to demonstrate a good number of the following skills and attributes:

- commitment to the school/trust and its mission
- personal integrity
- good understanding of the environment in which the school is operating and wider education policy
- good understanding of the role and legal responsibilities of the board and its members
- strong communication skills
- negotiation and diplomacy skills
- good organisational skills and the ability to prioritise
- ability to think strategically
- ability to chair meetings well
- ability to have courageous conversations and make courageous decisions
- ability to build and get the best out of a team
- capacity to process information quickly and understand relevant data, drawing valid conclusions
- ability and willingness to delegate and trust others

When deciding to nominate or vote for a governor or trustee as chair, length of service is not in itself a relevant factor. It is important that the candidate has the necessary qualities and skills to lead the team. Although a good understanding of the school and its context is important, this can be improved while in post, whereas skills such as relationship building and an ability to stay focused on the strategic priorities are more crucial. It is sometimes said that it is important to be well informed about education issues both locally and nationally; however, this is largely the preserve of the education professionals and the clerk can help a chair locate key information. Research tells us that personal qualities and leadership skills are most important in being a successful chair. You do not need to be knowledgeable about all aspects of the school or education policy, but you do need to understand the consequences of certain lines of thinking or action and be able to steer the board to make good decisions.

2.2 Electing the chair

In practice, most governing boards hold elections for chairs annually at the first meeting of each school year. The governing board decides the procedure for the election, but good practice suggests that:

- the clerk should act as returning officer
- members of the governing board should be given at least three weeks' notice of the election
- written nominations should be sought and returned in advance of the meeting
- candidates should be able to nominate themselves
- the governing board should ensure that anyone proposed for election is willing to serve
- those standing should all be given the opportunity to submit a statement in support of their candidacy and also speak about their candidacy at the meeting so that the other governors can make an informed decision
- even if there is only one candidate, a ballot should be held to enable a governing board to reject a nominee and open discussion about an alternative
- voting should be by secret ballot, not by show of hands (for many standalone academies, the model articles make this a requirement where the position is contested)
- the nominated candidate(s) must leave the room and cannot vote
- in the event of a tie, the ballot should be rerun

NGA has published a protocol for electing the chair, which members can access at www.nga.org.uk.

It is important that when the serving chair is standing again this is not taken as a foregone conclusion. The governing board has the option of re-electing the same person or replacing them with a new chair after consideration of what the school needs from the role. Often governors do not like to stand against an incumbent chair, but it is important that there are elections, rather than having to wait until a chair decides to retire from the role. Given that the chair has frequently been giving substantial time to the role, governors may find it difficult to vote against the incumbent, but when members are dissatisfied with her/his performance, governors must be courageous enough to put the interests of the pupils above those of the adult.

Governors/trustees should be reminded of the role and the qualities required to carry it out well. The chair's relationship with the headteacher/chief executive (see chapter 4.1) is vital, and although ultimately the senior executive has no more say than any other member of the board in the chair's appointment, their future working relationship is worth considering. Any successful candidate must be willing and able to both support and challenge the senior executive Those who have already chaired for three or four years should make plans for stepping down and communicate the timescale clearly to the rest of the board. When the chair is in that final year, it should be a priority for her/him to ensure there is someone to step forward the following September (see chapter 7.2) and that the governing board will continue to work well. This demonstrates the leadership required to leave governance in the school in good hands. Making oneself indispensable is not sustainable leadership.

2.3 The first weeks

All new chairs should expect induction activities to be available for their role. NGA thinks it should be an expectation that all new chairs and vice chairs who have not previously undertaken the DfE-funded Development for Chairs should seek out such a programme. NGA delivers Leading Governance and, working with partners, offers courses nationally. This programme also provides access to other chairs for sharing practice and forming a cluster group. For further information and to book a place, please see www.nga.org.uk/LeadingGovernance/Chairs.aspx

A new chair should:

- have a meeting with the head (see chapter 4.1)
- have a meeting with the clerk and discuss the arrangements for managing the business well (see chapter 6.3)
- if the circumstances permit, have a meeting with the outgoing chair
- have a meeting with the vice chair
- reflect as to her/his own understanding of the school, its context, challenges and priorities, and consider how best to fill any gaps
- consider whether the way in which the governing board does business enables the focus to be clearly on the strategic direction of the school and improving its performance
- seek the views of other governors and consider if their skills are being used to best effect
- make arrangements to access training specifically for new chairs of governing boards
- consider whether a mentor would be helpful: this could be an experienced chair from another school. The DfE designates some experienced chairs as national leaders of governance (NLGs) who, among other things, are able to offer support to new chairs of governors (see chapter 8)

In practice, we find some schools are without a vision and strategy to provide the direction and priorities for the school.

The first act of a new chair might therefore be to ascertain if the school strategy is fit for purpose. If it appears not to be, s/he should discuss this with the head and instigate the development of a vision and its agreement by the governing board, alongside a useful strategy document. For more information on developing a school strategy, see chapter 6.1.

The one exception to this may be the chair of an academy committee within a MAT, where the board of trustees has the responsibility for the MAT's overall strategy and will choose how much responsibility for the academy's strategy to delegate to its committee. The chair should be aware of that from the MAT's scheme of delegation.

Getting to know the rest of the board

It is good practice to have a vice chair, or possibly two. The vice chair(s) can be very important in sharing the leadership of the board, not only making the role of chair more manageable but also acting as a sounding board when there are challenges and opportunities to reflect on.

Almost all new chairs will come from within the governing board and therefore know the other members to a certain extent, but the new role can change the dynamics between people. S/he may not have had conversations with each of them individually, which can provide a useful perspective on the performance of the board and help to strengthen the team. The clerk should be able to provide you with their pen portraits, if the school doesn't keep them on the website alongside attendance records and conflicts of interest. Individual conversations will help you better understand their interests, motivations and commitment. It can also give you an opportunity to thank them for their contributions and emphasise the importance of the collective endeavour. At the same time it allows you to build bridges with governors/trustees you know less well or those who may not have supported you becoming chair, and to discuss how best to use their skills and knowledge.

Collaboration with other chairs

Many chairs across the country have described the value of meeting fellow chairs to share experiences. There may also be meetings and conferences for chairs of governing boards, as well as specific training sessions. You may want to make informal links with another local school and visit their governing board meeting to see how they manage their business, remembering that they might not have got it all right.

NGA strongly encourages chairs and governing boards to join and participate in their local independent governance association: contacts for the local associations can be found at www.nga.org.uk. Joining your governing board to

NGA itself also provides a route to receive information for governors, to hear from others and to collectively represent the governance perspective. NGA now holds virtual seminars for chairs: see www.nga.org.uk/events.

2.4 Managing your time

It may be that a new chair will need to spend more time initially, especially if s/he has not been a governor at the school for very long and needs to improve her/his knowledge of the school and develop relationships.

The State of School Governing national survey by NGA and the University of Bath in 2014 found that approximately two-thirds of chairs contributed more than 30 days a year and almost a quarter were spending more than 60 days a year. There are many similarities between chairs of school governing boards and charities (indeed academies are charitable companies). However, a 2016 survey by the Association of Chairs found just over half of chairs of charitable trusts were spending more than 48 days a year and just over a third were spending 60 days or more. Those most likely to spend over five days a month are chairs of the very smallest (a budget of under £10k: 41%) and the largest organisations (a budget of more than £5 million: 55%).

NGA then carried out further research, both interviews and completion of diaries, to investigate what this time was spent on, especially in 'good' and 'outstanding' schools. The findings were reported in 2016 as Time to Chair (see box opposite). The median time spent governing across the sample equated to around one working day per week, but with a considerable range, showing it was possible to chair in significantly less time, at least when there are no particularly challenging circumstances at the school. It is understandable that in a school that 'requires improvement' or where the head is struggling, more time might be necessary. In all schools there may well be some issues that demand more time – recruiting a new head, protracted complaints, joining a MAT – but where it is possible to distribute work among other governors, this should be encouraged.

Effective delegation was the most successful strategy for reducing the hours spent by the chair. For example, chairs need not volunteer to sit on panels for exclusions, or for staffing issues such as grievances, redundancy or disciplinaries. On the other hand, a chair will usually have something to offer both the appraisal panel for the headteacher (see chapter 3.3) and the recruitment panel for a new headteacher, but taking part in the recruitment of other senior leaders can reasonably be carried out by other governors.

The additional responsibilities that foundation and voluntary aided schools and academies have, not least as the direct employer of staff, can lead to a knock-on effect on the role of the chair. It is therefore especially important in these schools that chairs make use of the other members of the governing board. It is also important that the chair is extremely clear that staffing matters are the province initially of the head, and that governors do not become involved in operational matters (see chapter 1.2).

If you are finding your commitment is more than 30 days a year, it is advisable to sit down and work out what you are spending your time on, whether it is strictly necessary and/or whether it can be delegated to someone else. You may also consider having a co-chair: in other words, two individuals job-sharing the role (see chapter 2.5). NGA can offer advice if you and your board wish to consider this. It can also more easily allow governors in full-time employment to take on the role of chair.

Chairs run the risk of attempting more than they can reasonably manage, especially if their predecessor modelled that behaviour and other governors are content to leave too much to the chair. A chair should use every opportunity to delegate tasks to colleagues so as to leave themselves with enough time for what the chair alone can do, and also to engage the other members of the board meaningfully. Some chairs get into the habit of taking too many decisions themselves between meetings. This should not happen on a regular basis; chair's action (see chapter 5.6) should be used sparingly. It applies only where delaying a decision would be detrimental to pupils or staff, and if business is well planned such emergencies should arise infrequently. It might also be that the chair is being asked to make decisions or get involved with tasks that should lie with the senior leadership team.

2.5 Co-chairs

The DfE's statutory guidance for maintained schools states that more than one person can be appointed to the role of chair if the governing body believes that it is necessary and in the best interests of the school; academies have the same freedom. This sharing of the role can be a useful option, especially where governors have the necessary skills but not the time. Not only can this make the role practical for some people who would otherwise not be able to find the time, it can also strengthen the leadership of the board by having another person's valued judgment to draw on.

It may also be used for one year as a way of bringing in a new chair and enabling a long-serving chair to retire the following year. There is more guidance on co-chairing at www.nga.org.uk.

Key findings from NGA's 2016 Time to Chair research

1. The amount of time chairs spend on governance varies enormously. The governing board's context goes some way to explaining this, with exceptional events such as structural change taking up a considerable amount of the chair's time. However, in some cases chairs spent a significant amount of time on the day-to-day running of the governing board, suggesting that other factors are at play.

2. Governance is a thinking, not a doing, role and it is therefore unsurprising that overall the greatest amount of time was spent thinking about governance. Although some chairs set aside specific periods for reflection, thinking time was often not planned. Instead it happened naturally when doing something else such as preparing for a meeting, or even walking the dog.

3. For many chairs, balancing work, family life and governing was a challenge. Work emerged as the most influential factor, affecting both the amount of free time available to govern and flexibility to govern during the working day. Participants who were retired tended to spend more time on governing (with notable exceptions), suggesting that having more time available to govern often translates into spending more time on governance. Many of the chairs who were employed had developed strategies to help them manage their governance workload, suggesting that it is possible to undertake the role in less time if motivated to do so. The key challenge was that chairs needed to be flexible enough to react to unexpected events, such as the headteacher leaving or an Ofsted inspection.

4. Secondary chairs generally spent less time on governance than their primary colleagues: the median total time for primary chairs across the study period was approximately 20% more than that for secondary chairs, but the range for secondary chairs was also less, with the largest total time spent by a primary chair 40% more than by the secondary chair who spent the most time.

5. The most common time management strategy was delegation and sharing the workload across the governing board. In most cases this was ingrained into how the governing board operated and was a result of the board acting as a corporate body rather than the chair delegating from the top down. Where delegation was not effective, it was often the chair who picked up the slack and as a result became overburdened.

6. The vice chair was often underutilised, spending considerably less time on governing than the chair. This not only risked overburdening the chair, but also had implications for succession planning. The examples of where this relationship worked well provide a contrast and demonstrate the impact effective use of the vice chair can have on the governing board's effectiveness as a whole.

7. Streamlining the committee structure was another time-saving strategy that reduced duplication and the amount of time the chair spent in meetings. Few participants attended all committee meetings, and fewer still chaired all committee meetings. Indeed, some chairs made a proactive decision not to chair committees in order to build up the skills of other governors or trustees. This is better practice.

8. There were several examples of chairs overstepping the line between operational and strategic, spending time on activities such as helping with school trips, listening to children read, providing IT support in schools, undertaking book scrutinies and carrying out health and safety checks. In some cases these tasks constituted a separate voluntary role, but in other cases chairs were simply doing things that they should not do, which suggests that they did not understand the strategic remit of the governing board.

9. There appeared to be little appetite among chairs to introduce remuneration for the role. The most common argument against remuneration for chairs was that it would change the nature of the role and would attract people to the role for the 'wrong reasons'. The importance of governing for the 'right reasons' – giving something back and wanting the best for pupils – came across strongly.

10. Many of the participants who kept time diaries commented that the experience had helped them to reflect on their own practice, suggesting that other chairs would benefit from undertaking a similar self-evaluation exercise.

Key findings from NGA's 2020 Time to Chair a Multi Academy Trust

1. Chairing a MAT, on average, takes just under 50 days a year; however, there is significant variation in the time taken to perform the role, with the difference between the individuals giving the most and least amount of time being more than 1,100 hours a year (or more than 150 days).

2. Over half of MAT chairs are retired or semi-retired and spend significantly longer on their governance role, devoting almost a third more time than those in full-time employment.

3. MAT chairs were mixed on whether they were content with the time it took them to chair their MAT; however, few were considering resigning as a result of this sacrifice.

4. Despite limited evidence that the size of a MAT affected the chair's reported time commitment, over 80% of MAT chairs felt that the time commitment of chairing their trust had increased as a result of their MAT growing in size.

5. Delegation was the most cited strategy used for reducing and managing the time it takes to chair a MAT, but varying practices surrounding Scheme of Delegations (SoDs) have meant that MAT chairs are undertaking a wide variety of tasks that could be delegated elsewhere.

6. Just over a quarter (28%) reported having not put any strategies in place to manage their time more effectively, despite their hefty workload.

7. 56% did not have a succession plan and some chairs noted a reluctance from others on the board to step forward into the chairing role in the future.

8. The diversity of MAT chairs is also limited, underrepresented by females and in particular individuals from black, Asian and other ethnic minority backgrounds.

9. Most MAT chairs are present on more than one tier of governance and just under half (41%) govern at all three tiers (ie they are trust members, trustees and attend academy committee meetings in some capacity); this contributed significantly to their workload.

10. Apart from attending academy committee meetings, the most time-consuming activity for MAT chairs was meeting their CEO and other members of the executive team.

11. Just over one-third of MAT chairs had not undertaken any governance training within the last year and many cited time constraints as the reason for this.

12. While MAT chairs seem aware of the arguments for remuneration, the vast majority are against paying those performing their role.

Tips for making the role of chair manageable

- make your regular face-to-face meetings with the headteacher/chief executive monthly; communicate by email and phone between meetings

- work efficiently with the clerk, drawing on their services fully (see chapter 6.3); do not carry out administrative functions

- share tasks (such as chairing task and finish groups, liaising with the local authority or academy trust/ committees, developing community links, researching issues, inducting and mentoring new governors) around the governing board, particularly with the vice chair

- consider whether you need to attend every committee meeting, and whether each committee is required (see chapter 6.2)

- delegate to the headteacher wherever possible, for example, updating policies and decisions concerning performance-related pay for staff

- ensure the headteacher understands the governance role as regards recruitment (ie does not request governors to interview staff other than senior leaders) and is competent to deal with staffing matters; these should not be the province of the chair, and only at the end of the process should they become a matter for a panel of governors

- do not sit on panels for exclusions or staffing issues such as grievances, redundancy or disciplinaries

- suggest that the complaints policy does not include a stage for review by the chair alone; there is no need and eliminating it can save substantial time

- if the time required has become unmanageable and may lead to you having to stop governing, you could consider cutting down on any other voluntary activities you are doing in the school in addition to governance, such as reading with pupils or helping with school trips (this also adds clarity to your role)

- if you govern within a MAT, do not govern at more than one level ie have separation between the trust members, the board of trustees and the academy committee/LGB

- if it is still proving too time-consuming, think about having co-chairs

So what next?

In this guide, we have identified five elements to the role of chair of governors that are covered in the following chapters:

- leading and developing the team of governors
- building the relationship with the headteacher and ensuring accountability
- leading school improvement
- leading the business of the governing board
- ensuring a succession plan

Leading and developing the team

A successful board is essentially a group that has a full set of complementary skills, experience and knowledge that, when used effectively, can deliver results. A team becomes more than just a collection of people when a strong sense of shared commitment and values creates synergy, thus generating performance greater than the sum of the performance of its individual members. It is the chair's leadership that helps to achieve successful team working and a competent board.

An effective chair builds an effective team by:

- displaying integrity and being trustworthy
- ensuring the team has the range of skills required to carry out its role
- ensuring all members understand their role
- ensuring all members of the governing board undertake appropriate training, especially induction
- ensuring that governors feel valued, and encouraging their individual development
- championing team and board development
- setting the culture of the governing board, balancing and valuing both the support and the challenge elements
- delegating roles and tasks, ensuring all governors are fully involved
- being willing to let others take the lead according to their particular strengths and the situation
- having courageous conversations with governors who are not contributing positively to the team
- giving a clear lead in evaluating the governing board's work and her/his own

DfE competencies for a chair: part 2

- takes a strategic view of the skills that the board needs, identifies gaps and takes action to ensure these are filled
- ensures everyone understands why they have been recruited and what role they play in the governance structure
- ensures new people are helped to understand their non-executive leadership role, the role of the board, and the vision and strategy of the organisation, enabling them to make a full contribution
- leads discussions and decisions about what functions to delegate
- creates an atmosphere of open, honest discussion where it is safe to constructively challenge conventional wisdom
- creates a sense of inclusiveness where each member understands their individual contribution to the collective work of the board
- builds a close, open and supportive working relationship with the vice chair that respects the differences in their roles
- promotes and fosters a supportive working relationship between the board, clerk/governance professional, executive leaders, staff of the organisation and external stakeholders

- identifies and cultivates leadership within the board
- recognises individual and group achievements, not just in relation to the board but in the wider organisation
- sets challenging development goals and works effectively with the board to meet them
- leads performance reviews of the board and its committees
- undertakes open and honest conversations with board members about their performance and development needs and, if appropriate, commitment or tenure
- recognises and develops talent in board members and ensures they are provided with opportunities to realise their potential
- creates a culture in which board members are encouraged to take ownership of their own development
- promotes and facilitates coaching, development, mentoring and support for all members of the board
- is able to recognise when the board or an individual member is not behaving as expected and take appropriate action to address this
- actively invites feedback on their own performance as chair

An effective leader creates the conditions that engage others in working together to achieve their common purpose. S/he inspires the team and generates the energy to achieve the goals. Most governors will be self-motivating, but the chair will need to create a climate that maintains that motivation. Individual chairs will have their own style and ways of working. To some extent, as with any other leadership role, there is no single way to chair. However, there are some approaches and behaviours that will not foster good board dynamics and it is important that chairs are aware of what these are. A 360-degree review is invaluable for understanding this, and is available from NGA (see chapter 2.4).

3.1 Building the team's capability

The chair should be much concerned with building a diverse team of governors with varied knowledge, backgrounds and skills, who together can address all the needs of the governance role. A governing board will be stronger and better able to challenge each other and the school's leaders if its members have a variety of views and experience.

Diversity is an area that some chairs of school governing boards tend to neglect, rather than thinking of it as one of their responsibilities. NGA supports the Young Governors' Network and the Everyone On Board campaign, which encourages Black, Asian and minority ethnic (BAME) and young people to volunteer as school governors. Both young and BAME people are currently underrepresented on governing boards.

NGA has made nine pledges to improve the ethnic diversity of governing boards and to promote the governing board's role in ensuring a culture of equality and inclusion throughout the school or trust.

Having diverse and balanced governing boards that reflect the communities they serve will ensure that different insights and perspectives shape conversations, and that thinking is robustly challenged, resulting in better decision-making and outcomes for all pupils. For more information see nga.org.uk/everyone-on-board.

Conducting a skills audit

A skills audit should be carried out on a regular basis and the results used when considering training needs, committee responsibilities and succession, as well as when filling any vacancies on the governing board. The majority of governing boards do conduct a skills audit.

All governors should have relevant skills and experience, but the governing board needs to collectively bring a range of backgrounds and competencies appropriate to its wide range of responsibilities. The chair needs to consider seriously

> " Good governance needs a range of voices. And that was powerfully on display in the video we have just seen – and I champion the work NGA is doing, through your Everyone On Board campaign, to encourage more diversity – and for more women in leadership roles. Governing and trust boards should reflect the communities they serve. So, I want to urge people from different backgrounds, different professions, to come forward – to offer up their time, energy, skills, and expertise. Parent governors continue to be crucial and I'd like to see more young people get involved, more people from black and ethnic minority communities, more people from right across society with the ability and experience to lead. "

Damian Hinds MP, then secretary of state for education, at NGA's summer conference, June 2018

whether the governing board has the full set of skills and knowledge it needs to do its job properly. As well as integrity and high ethical standards, the essential skills include:

- communication skills (including active listening)
- understanding data and the ability to draw conclusions from a range of evidence
- the ability to question well
- softer relationship-building skills that encourage team working, facilitate good decision-making and ensure good working relationships with a range of different stakeholders

Many governors will have more than one of these skills, but if the chair feels there is a deficit of any of these across the team or an imbalance in terms of the strengths of the team, s/he will need to ensure the governing board discusses this at its next meeting in order to rectify the situation.

All volunteers need to have a commitment to improving education for all pupils, the ability to work in a professional manner as part of a team, and take collective responsibility for decisions.

There is a wide range of expertise that can be useful on a governing board: financial management and accountancy; legal expertise; human resources; property/estates management; procuring and contracting services; project management; organisational change management; equal opportunities; special needs; quality assurance and service improvement; risk management; health and safety; marketing and public relations; IT. These are included here not because governors will undertake these tasks, but because this experience enables them to understand the issues and analyse information, thus supporting the leadership team with advice, asking challenging questions, and meeting their legal and financial obligations.

Some leadership teams do like to seek free expertise from their governors, in addition to their governance role. It is important that the chair understands the difference between giving time as a governor and the option of donating additional time to other tasks. Governors must not feel that they are under any obligation to volunteer for tasks over and above the time taken by governing. We know of lawyers who have left governing boards because they felt they were being used for free legal advice on a range of issues, rather than as a governor. Furthermore, this can cause conflicts of interest and so is best avoided.

No governing board is likely to include all of these areas of expertise, but the list can be considered if a relevant vacancy occurs. All schools and chairs themselves are greatly helped by building the number of active and able governors. Some chairs – and indeed local authorities, foundations and trusts – have been more concerned with simply filling vacancies, and have not been proactive in making sure all skills and backgrounds are represented around the table.

In January 2017, the Department for Education (DfE) published a competency framework for those governing. NGA incorporated these requirements into our model skills audits, which are reviewed annually – one for those governing in a single school and one for those governing a group of schools. There is an accompanying matrix at http://www.nga.org.uk/Competency-Framework-for-Governance.

Recruiting skilled people

Once the required skills have been identified, contacts need to be made to encourage those with the skills to apply for the role. It is good practice to include a role description that spells out clearly the expectations – for example, in terms of time and training – as part of the information sent to the prospective governor prior to the interview. NGA has developed a generic role description for governors and another for trustees, which can be found in our induction guides Welcome to Governance and Welcome to a Multi Academy Trust respectively, or at https://www.nga.org.uk/Knowledge-Centre/Governance-structure-roles-and-responsibilities.aspx.

A wide range of organisations can be approached: local employers; Chambers of Commerce; public services with whom the school works; community organisations; and further and higher education establishments. Other schools can also be a rich source of volunteers. It is very good continuing professional development (CPD) for middle leaders to volunteer as a governor at another school. If suitable

inspiring governance | The school governance recruitment and support service

Inspiring Governance is a FREE DfE-funded online service connecting schools and trusts in England with skilled volunteers in their area who are interested in becoming a school governor/trustee or future chair. Once appointed, an Inspiring Governance volunteer receives access to free support, expert guidance and e-learning from NGA for 12 months.

www.inspiringgovernance.org

volunteers cannot be found through local links, there are two national volunteer banks for school governors and an Academy Ambassadors scheme that headhunts academy trustees. Further information on all of these can be found at www.nga.org.uk.

Every category of governor can be approached in this way with a little encouragement, but there is perhaps most scope for this approach with co-opted, local authority, foundation and sponsor governors. Even with parent governor elections, when seeking nominations it is essential to include information about the role and it is possible to state that the governing board is ideally looking for someone with a particular background or experience. At the same time, it is necessary to appreciate that not all school communities include parents with professional backgrounds, and it is important to value parents' experience of the school. Parent governors do bring – albeit partial – knowledge of the school that external governors do not and this can be invaluable in informing questions to ask school leaders.

For categories that do not require elections, once applications are received, there should be an interview with the chair and at least one other governor, where the role is explained and the skills and competencies being sought are discussed. It would not usually be the role of the headteacher to interview for the board that holds her/him to account. However, if the board is currently weak, it can be appropriate for the lead executive to offer support in developing it, but this is an indication that the chair is not fulfilling his/her role well. If a governing board decides not to take up the offer of a volunteer, it is good practice to offer feedback about why not. There is a culture in some schools of only co-opting people already known to the school community, but while local networks can be a useful route to finding willing volunteers, this can also create 'group think', which acts against a lively culture of challenge and self-review. It is important to treat all approaches in the same way, and not deter unknown offers. Diversity of thought and ideas comes from a board made up of diverse individuals.

If a governing board does not have a member with good financial management skills and there are no vacancies to which such a governor can be recruited, the chair may want to suggest that an associate member is appointed to cover this important area of expertise. Associate members are people appointed by a governing board to a committee – they are not governors, although they are entitled to attend governing board meetings. Academies can also appoint individuals who are not trustees to sit on board committees, although in this case they do not have an automatic right to attend trustee meetings.

Induction of new governors and trustees

Governors and trustees need to understand both their role and the institution they are governing. The chair should ensure that new governors, including staff governors, are inducted well. To cover the role and responsibilities of being a governor, NGA produces Welcome to Governance, and Welcome to a Multi Academy Trust (MAT), a guide for new trustees.

NGA recommends that all new governors be provided with an induction pack that includes:

- Welcome to Governance/Welcome to a MAT (as applicable) – GOLD members of NGA will receive a copy when we are provided with the details of the new governor/trustees, as will those volunteers recruited through Inspiring Governance and Academy Ambassadors

- the school's instrument of governance/academy's articles of association (and in a MAT, the scheme of delegation to any academy-level governance)

- a list of the members of the governing board

- a calendar of scheduled meetings

- a list of the governing board's committees and their terms of reference

- the school's prospectus (if it has one)

- the trust's/school's strategy (or if it has not been developed, the school development/improvement plan) and the most recent school self-evaluation

- information about the performance standards in the school(s)

- the governing board code of practice

In addition to school-based induction, it is advisable to offer more formal training to a new governor, usually by an external source. Face-to-face induction training will be offered by most local authorities and may have been purchased as part of a governor support services package. Most MATs also offer induction training, but it is still useful to meet governors from other schools outside MAT. Training can also be accessed effectively as virtual face-to-face sessions or via e-learning platforms such as NGA's Learning Link, which contains eight specific induction modules as well as many more covering the range of board responsibilities.

The chair should make a point of introducing new governors to their colleagues, and offer them a mentor from the experienced governors, perhaps the vice chair.

Knowing the school or trust

It is critical that governors have a good knowledge of the school itself. The chair needs to encourage all governors to engage appropriately with the school, its stakeholders and its data, and ensure that all meetings receive reports from senior leaders that are fit for purpose. Governors and trustees must be visible to stakeholders, and visiting the school is one method of achieving this. Chapter 5.1 has more information on getting to know the school.

The situation is very different for trustees of a MAT, where visits will play a smaller part in getting to know the schools they govern. The chair needs to ensure that the mechanism for the academy committees to feed information to the board of trustees is working well. This is essential for trustees to understand their schools, but many MATs have struggled to set up effective communication with academy committees. NGA can advise on ways of doing this.

Continuing training and development

The continuing professional development of the head and staff is a key concern of the governing board; CPD is also important for the governing board itself. The chair should take a lead role in stressing the importance of CPD, ensuring that all governors have had the benefit of appropriate CPD, and setting an example by undertaking her/his own CPD. Research from other sectors has found that outstanding board chairs spend a significant amount of time developing, advising and mentoring other board members.

In terms of succession planning (see chapter 7.2), it is important that the chair encourages possible future chairs of the board to participate in a leadership development programme: some programmes are being funded by the DfE including NGA's Leading Governance.

There should be a committed element within the school budget for governor and trustee training and development. NGA is concerned about the low level of resources often allocated in school budgets for CPD of the governing board. It is counterproductive to unduly restrict expenditure aimed at improving the effectiveness of governance.

Effective CPD should be planned to include both internal and external providers. Some training may be offered for clusters of schools, or the chair may want to consider this as a way of both cutting costs and sharing experiences with another governing board. It should consist of a manageable programme, with a range of activities for individual and small groups of governors, and occasional activities for full governing boards working in partnership with leadership teams. As there are also practical issues about getting to training sessions, e-learning (such as NGA's Learning Link) can also be offered for governors to use when it suits them. It can be productive to allocate half an hour before board meetings for a training session for all members; this could be provided by one of its members, one of the executive team or through an e-learning module. The chair must also bear in mind that for some governors who are not highly educated, the prospect of accessing training may be frightening or culturally difficult.

Retaining good people

> **❝** The tides of trusteeship carry boards in the wrong direction from strategy towards operations, from long-term challenges to immediate concerns, from collective action to individual initiatives… most boards just drift with the tides and therefore as a result trustees are little more than high-powered, well-intentioned people engaged with low-level activities. **❞**

Chait, Holland & Taylor in Improving the Performance of Governing Boards

The chair cannot think the job is done when s/he has assembled an impressive, diverse team of people who have agreed to govern; s/he needs to ensure their time and skills are used well. The rest of this guide should help you to do this, but you do need to be aware of warning signs, and when a governor leaves, conduct an exit interview (see NGA's guidance centre for more detail).

3.2 Creating a healthy culture

> **❝** Chairs should encourage governors to work as an effective team, building their skills, knowledge and experience. They need to ensure that all governors are actively contributing relevant skills and experience, participating constructively in meetings, and playing their part in the work of any committees. It is their role to make sure every governor knows what is expected of them and receives appropriate induction and training. It is for the chair to have honest conversations, as necessary, if governors are not pulling their weight. **❞**

Departmental advice for school leaders and governing bodies of maintained schools and management committees of PRUs January 2014

An effective team

- Shares a sense of purpose and direction. Its members know what they are there for and what they are trying to achieve. They share common goals and are all pulling in the same direction.

- Understands the roles and responsibilities of the team, and its members are clear about what is expected of them as individuals.

- Communicates well. People listen to each other, and where there are differences of opinion, these are dealt with openly and honestly.

- Trusts and values its members. When things do not go well, individuals are not blamed but the team thinks about how they could work together to improve the situation.
- Manages its meetings well in order to get the job done.
- Reflects on how well it is working and changes its practice to improve, for example, by discussing its effectiveness once a year.

The values of the school should bind all those involved together and be modelled by the governing board. This then sets the culture for the whole organisation. A chair of an academy committee within a MAT may have less latitude for developing a distinctive culture as the values and ethos should be set by the board of trustees, and in cases where s/he has concerns may want to draw on support from within the MAT. It is good practice for the chair of the MAT board to meet with the chairs of academy committees/LGBs.

The chair will recognise when individual behaviours are not as expected, but sometimes it is more difficult to see when the behaviour of the team as a whole is no longer contributing to high performance. This could be because the board has become too comfortable or because the challenging circumstances of the school or trust have added to the board's anxiety. It could also be that the behaviour of the chair is inhibiting the team performance; perhaps the chair is doing too much and not involving others sufficiently or is not tackling tensions before they become conflicts. Chapter 3.4 covers the behaviours of a high-performing board.

Building trust

Trust is a product of positive human interactions and is built in two ways:
- Cognitive trust, through professional capability and integrity demonstrated by track record and actions
- Affective trust, an emotional bond based on receipt of genuine care and concern

It is essential in building all the relationships involved in governance, between members of the board, between the board and the executive, and between both the board and the leadership with the stakeholders, in particular staff and parents. Once trust is instilled, then openness, the sharing of knowledge and shared ownership, follows.

Track record	– demonstrating professional capability and integrity
Reliability	– sticking to commitments and being consistent
Understanding	– listening and appreciating others
Sincerity	– showing genuine care and concern
Transparency	– being open, honest and accountable

Code of conduct

NGA recommends that all governing boards have a code of conduct that explains the role and the expectations. NGA has developed a model code that we suggest governing boards adapt and governors/trustees sign every year. The code is available at www.nga.org.uk. Most governing boards have adopted a code of conduct, and we suggest the chair introduces this practice if it is not already in place.

Delegation

“ The chair is the architect of the board and it is up to him or her to ensure that the division of labour is effective. ”

The Fish Rots from the Head: developing effective board directors by Bob Garratt

Delegation is a key task for any leader, but in this context it also has the advantage of distributing the leadership itself across the team. Chairs should encourage the participation of other governors by encouraging those with the relevant skills to chair committees and lead on aspects of business. If a governor does not have one of the skills necessary for a task, the chair should suggest training or another form of development to help that governor contribute effectively.

The chair has the delicate task of keeping an eye on how governors are coping with the work they undertake, and should be ready to encourage and praise, to persuade colleagues to undergo suitable training and, if necessary, to relieve them of tasks.

Plainly, the chair has a better chance of building and maintaining an effective team of governors if s/he is approachable, readily accessible to other governors, takes their concerns and enthusiasms seriously and, as far as possible, works to maintain good personal relationships. Governors tend to respond well to chairs who shoulder their own responsibilities and at the same time show that they value the contributions of their colleagues, including challenge from other members of the board.

It is not unusual for the chair to take on a large portion of the work that has to be done by governors between meetings. However, this is not a sustainable method of working, nor does it develop other board members. It can be particularly tricky for chairs who are themselves in employment, and while there will inevitably be some tasks best suited to the chair, these are fewer than might first be thought. Many can also be given to the clerk to carry out. See below for the role of committee chairs, and also review what is expected from any link or specialist governors. Appeal panels, whether for staff issues (grievances, pay, disciplinary or redundancy), pupil exclusions or admissions, can also be dealt with by other governors.

In terms of its formal responsibilities and duties, the board has to decide what it is delegating to committees and individuals. Terms of reference or, as these are likely to be called within a MAT, the scheme of delegation, must be understood by all members of the board. It must be remembered that by and large individual governors do not make decisions; the board is a corporate entity. The tasks between meetings often concern gathering and analysing information or checking that actions from the previous meeting are being progressed. It is important that any terms of reference or schemes of delegation make sense on paper; don't build a system around who you have on the board and what they prefer.

Vice chairs

Every governing board should have a vice chair who can step in for the chair. When the vice chair acts as chair, s/he has the same role, the same casting vote and the same responsibility to act in tune with the wishes of the governing board. Clearly it is extremely important that the chair maintains a close working relationship with the vice chair and considers how the vice chair might be fully informed, for example, attending some of the meetings with the head. In many governing boards the vice chair is an underused resource.

In addition, the role of vice chair offers plenty of scope for the development of leadership skills and could be involved in a number of ways, such as:

- taking on a specific responsibility, for example committee chair or development of governors
- chairing particular agenda items or some full governing board meetings
- acting as a mentor for new governors
- sharing some of the tasks, for example interviewing for senior leaders
- being part of the team that undertakes the head's annual appraisal (this is particularly advisable if the chair is not involved) or acting as the appeal
- undertaking exit interviews of senior staff and of board members

In order to emphasise the corporate nature of governance, to prevent a common perception by other governors that the head and chair are too close, and to increase the chances of succession of both the vice chair and the deputy head, it is helpful to consider having some meetings at school, at least termly, with all four present.

If a vice chair has no intention of volunteering for the role of chair in the future, consider having two vice chairs, one a longer-serving governor and the other a potential future chair (see chapter 7.2 on succession planning).

Committee chairs

The majority of boards choose to have some committees (see chapter 6.2), in particular one to undertake the detailed monitoring of educational outcomes and a second overseeing management of resources, both financial and staff. Sub-committees are probably unnecessary for academy committees/LGBs, but the chair will still need to ensure that the members of the committee understand and can interrogate the data.

It is not good practice for the chair of the board to chair a committee, but the chair will need to consider who has the skills to lead these two key areas of scrutiny and approach them to discuss them being nominated for the role. Although the chair must have an understanding of both these fundamental governing board duties, the detailed and more forensic exploration and interrogation of the data – both educational and financial – should be covered by other members of the board. This can be in conjunction with the chair and the vice chair, one of whom might work with the committee chair to provide support, challenge and a sounding board.

The committee chair will play largely the same role for the committee and its subject areas that the chair of the board does overall, not only in meetings but also in terms of discussions with senior leaders and setting agendas with the clerk.

If the vice chair of the board chairs one of the committees, the chair of the board needs to make sure there are others on the committee who understand the subject area. The detailed financial or educational knowledge should not be held by only a few people. The chair of the board must ensure that all its members have the necessary knowledge of the school's data and that there are sufficient members who have detailed knowledge and the ability to ask incisive questions. Those with the more expert knowledge may be suitable candidates to chair the committee, but equally may not have the right qualities to chair and may be better asking the questions rather than steering the discussion. The chair of the board needs to know the members well enough to make those judgment calls as to what roles suit best, and encourage others to step forward.

Expenses

Chairs are likely to incur some out-of-pocket expenses. All governing boards should have an expenses policy for governors, and chairs should take the lead on ensuring that this is the case and encouraging their fellow governors to claim. A model expenses policy can be found in NGA's knowledge centre. NGA is sometimes told that such an expenses policy is unnecessary or undesirable because the school cannot afford to pay expenses. However, no matter how small the school, governor expenses will be a tiny proportion of its budget and any school that values its governors will not hesitate to make such a budgetary allowance readily available, clear and transparent. It is important to ensure that the possibility of incurring expenses does not deter those on low incomes or with childcare costs from becoming governors. Costs of training, including travel, should also be available.

The culture in meetings

The chair is in the very influential position of being able to establish a way of doing business that reinforces both the strategic role of the board and the collective nature of corporate decision-making. A chair should encourage all governors/trustees to contribute at meetings. There are some who attend meetings but remain silent; on the other hand, there may be a dominant personality who speaks too often or in such a way that makes others feel unable to disagree.

A healthy debate triggered by some difference of opinion, especially before important decisions are taken, should be encouraged in governing board meetings. It must be clear that the decision is not a foregone conclusion or sewn up in advance. Indeed, boards should not always be comfortable places; those that are cosy are likely to be underperforming. Complacent boards can get into bad habits, which will not generally be noticed by longstanding members but may be perceived by new members or observers. The chair must make sure challenge by new members or visitors is taken seriously and not dismissed with "this is how we do things here". Indeed challenge from whichever direction should be listened to as concerns being brushed under the carpet will lead to dysfunction, mistrust and potentially conflict. Differences of opinion about how to achieve a strategic priority will test a proposed approach thoroughly; unanimity in the first instance would be a concern for a chair. As well as different stances among the board, there should be a healthy tension with the board being aspirational and the headteacher bringing in what is achievable. The chair needs to be skilled at acknowledging and understanding different perspectives, and capable of finding common ground.

However, all discussions must of course be conducted in a professional manner. Where governors and staff are strongly committed to the vision and ethos of the school, debates can become passionate, but the chair's role is to ensure that they remain relevant and constructive, rather than becoming overheated. Good chairing requires emotional intelligence: self-awareness, self-control, empathy and an awareness of relationships and their power dynamics. It is important to be able to remain focused on the goal while being flexible in what tactics may achieve them.

A culture of blame must also be avoided; the board needs to learn lessons from poor performance or problems, without being accusatory or crossing into issues that should be addressed in staff performance management.

Some governors might have a particular personal agenda; if this is brought up, the chair must ensure the meeting returns to the matter in hand and is not diverted from its agenda. When this is a parent who has their own children's particular interests at heart, it is important that s/he is reminded that the board is governing in the interests of all the pupils, but this also suggests that induction was not as thorough as it should have been. However, it can occur with any governor who manages to raise a particular issue repeatedly. If it persists, a conversation outside the meeting between the chair and that governor is likely to be necessary.

Straying into the operational management must not be tolerated, and it is the chair's role to cut off those contributions swiftly with a reminder of the board's role. The chair can expect the vice chair's support on this, but if it is a common occurrence, discussions need to be had outside the meeting, probably including the headteacher and the clerk if more than one governor is involved, about the best approach to rectify this. This might require training or a governance review.

Unhealthy board behaviours a chair needs to address include:

- remote, disinterested, or distracted by a phone or other electronic device
- rudeness, disapproval, aggression (as opposed to assertiveness) or bullying displayed
- dysfunctionally polite boards that avoid debate
- emotional outbursts, overheated arguments, or disagreements becoming personal
- domination by one or two individuals (even if one of them is the headteacher)
- an over-deferential board (see also chapter 5.4 on challenge and questioning)

- questioning that is hostile or repetitive
- getting involved in operational detail
- no comment, question or disagreement expressed during meetings (compounded by relaying unhappiness to the chair after the meeting)
- being unwilling to accept a majority decision and/or trying to reopen decisions previously made

3.3 Exercising influence

The ability to influence others is central to being a successful governor or trustee, and even more so for the chair. The chair needs to influence other board members, the headteacher, other stakeholders and external organisations. Being influential can come from having a position of authority, although influence without executive power is not as clear cut. It can also come from the networks or associations you bring to the role. The ability to persuade others will come from your behaviours: how effectively you listen and consider alternative ideas, and your ability to marshal clear, credible arguments. In time, you will build up a track record and earn a reputation; those who respect you are more likely to be influenced by you, but it should be perfectly possible to have a fundamental disagreement without losing respect for one another.

High support

Supporters club	Partners or critical friends
"We're here to support the head!"	"We share everything – good or bad!"

Low challenge   **High challenge**

Abdicators	Adversaries
"We leave it to the professionals!"	"We keep a very close eye on the staff!"

Low support

Based on page 9 of Research Matters No 20, Summer 2003, NSIN, Institute of Education, University of London

You will also develop your own style in this role, which may well differ from the way in which you carry out other roles. Your style may appeal to some people more than others, who may then be less receptive to you. But more than in any other role of power, the chair must be conscious of the collective nature of the governing task. An authoritarian, dominant or command-and-control style is completely unsuitable to the role of chair. Your style must also sit well with the ethos and culture of the organisation.

As chair, you are not trying to win every argument, but to enable the board to deliberate and reach a decision. Achieving the balance between intervening with your own judgment and facilitating others to use theirs can be a challenge but is one of the most important aspects of the chair's role. S/he must judge when to bring a discussion to an end without avoiding a concluding decision or action. After contentious decisions, the chair needs to be able to hold the alliance together for the greater good and prevent those in the minority from feeling alienated.

Courageous conversations

It is not uncommon for a chair to consider their governing board as having half a dozen active governors and an equal or smaller number who are variously described as 'passengers', 'sleepers' or 'dead wood'. If the board is managing despite their lack of contribution, there may be too many places on the board, and reconstitution should be considered.

However, lack of effort by some governors may be putting a strain on those who are actively engaged, and this must be tackled. It is the chair's job to discuss issues that are affecting their ability to contribute; there will be a wide range of reasons, including sensitive ones concerning health or other personal circumstances. There may be members who are exceptionally busy at work or have so many other commitments that they miss meetings. The chair should consult the clerk about the attendance record of governors, and be ready to tackle poor attendees well before there is any question of their disqualification for non-attendance. On the other hand, the atmosphere in the meetings, the dynamics between members of the board, misunderstanding of the role or a lack of confidence could be the cause.

It is helpful to have set out the expectations in a code that has been agreed by all, but this does not guarantee appropriate behaviour. Difficult as it may seem, the chair needs to talk to any members of the board whose behaviour does not seem to accord with the code or is in some way detracting from the effective functioning of the board. These conversations not only reinforce expectations but can help the chair to understand how another member might perceive their leadership style. It may be that those who are not contributing find the active members at the centre too dominating and territorial.

Some chairs have used board reconstitution to remove difficult members or those who are not contributing. This will not suit all situations, although it does seem easier to instil a team ethos and trust within smaller boards, which tend to have fewer disruptive members. However, it is important not to replace the awkward squad with a group of such like-minded people that there is no longer a wide range of challenge. Sometimes the awkward squad is right, or at least has a point worthy of consideration.

Introducing recommended limits on terms of office is a simple way of ensuring there is change within the board, preventing relationships becoming too close for too long and ensuring independent thought. It stops long-standing members taking challenging situations personally and means succession planning (see chapter 7.2), which is often neglected, must be taken seriously.

Dealing with factions, disputes and conflicts

There can also be unhelpful behaviours that are not just related to one member but suggest the board as a whole might not be working as well as it should. Vigorous debate is a sign of a thriving team, but a problem arises when disagreements within meetings begin to affect relationships. The chair needs to be alert to any warning signals that mistrust is developing, including suspicions expressed about others' attitudes or motivations, and briefing against others outside meetings. As difficult as this can be, it is the chair's role to tackle any dysfunction within the team. Factionalism within a governing board can be hugely diverting and energy sapping.

Participants are likely to be constantly assessing where others stand, both inside and outside meetings. This is part of the process of weighing up the situation and coming to a conclusion. Discussing issues between meetings informally can be very useful preparation but becomes a problem if a clique is seen as developing from which other members of the board feel excluded. Some members of the board will know each other in other ways, but this is only a problem if those loyalties, whether professional or personal, interfere with their ability to come to an objective judgment.

Conflict on the board can arise from differences between or among individual members or factions. Varying perspectives can sometimes seem irreconcilable and diverting. An effective board chair can be influential in managing the conflict and must attempt to do so. This involves achieving a balance between encouraging the airing of conflicting views and knowing when to step in to make sure that the board can achieve its business by making necessary and timely decisions. The chair should be careful not to add to conflict by making peremptory rulings and cutting off discussion prematurely, but will set the tone and help the governing board reach a productive resolution.

Chairs need to take action before cliques are formed and disagreements become protracted and personal, distracting the board from its core functions. A quiet conversation might avoid escalation to formal discussions with the board and decisions to suspend or remove any member. Appeals to the interests of the school and its pupils may well have to be made, but if the protagonists are making personal attacks on others or perceiving personal slights on themselves, they may no longer be amenable to such informal mediation.

Tremendous judgment, tact and diplomacy may be needed to explore fears, avoiding speculation and hearsay, in order to reach a resolution that allows the governing board to function well in a spirit of cooperation, openness and respect to achieve common goals. Better still, avoid it developing. Whether or not a chair is worried about factions on the governing board, team-building exercises can help to promote cohesion. Individual reviews can also be helpful, albeit time-consuming in the first instance, but well worth the investment in the medium term. The chair will gain individuals' views on the board dynamics and have the opportunity to emphasise that all views are valued.

The chair can also expect the head to raise with her/him any concerns about the actions or attitudes of the governing board or particular governors. There can be times when conflicts arise either between the governing board and the headteacher, or between some of the school staff and some governors. Again, it is the chair's job to deal with such matters. These discussions will often be difficult and the chair might want to seek the counsel of the vice chair, or a mentor from another governing board.

Literature from the third sector suggests that differences between the board of trustees and the executive often concern the boundaries of each other's roles and responsibilities. A common area of tension with school staff can be when a governor misunderstands the role, for example, a governor not adhering to protocols during a visit to the school, getting too involved with operational matters or misunderstanding the position in relation to their own child. The chair must not hesitate to address such issues in an appropriate way. If disputes become untenable, external facilitation might be necessary.

Modes of board behaviour: the 5 S's

An alternative way of considering different modes of board behaviour has been developed by Julia Unwin CBE, a former charity commissioner. She identified five modes in which high-performing boards operate and considers that while very good boards use all of these modes, excellent boards know which they are using and when.

Support

To encourage the executive and enable them to do their work, boards in support mode say:

- Have you got what you need to do that?
- We really ought to celebrate that.
- We really can't allow you to be treated like that.

Stewardship

To protect and conserve their assets, boards guarding an organisation's money and good name for the beneficiaries of tomorrow as well as today say:

- But will the money be here to continue this in five years' time?
- Are we giving away our intellectual property too easily?
- Is the reputational risk too great if we do this?
- Is this really in the interest of our current and future pupils?

Scrutiny

To hold the executive to account, boards that are scrutinising propositions put to them or examining process say:

- But this really doesn't make sense: why do you do it like this? Or: Why would we want to change our services in this way?
- What are the implications of doing it like this or doing it differently?
- What alternatives did you consider and why?
- What are the risks of not doing it like this?
- I don't think you have made the case that...

Boards face risks when they need to be making strategy, but are in fact offering support, or when they are so busy husbanding the resource of the organisation that they don't offer that vital sense of stretch. Although developed for boards in the third sector, these five modes apply to school governing boards too.

Strategy

Before making the big decisions that affect the future direction of an organisation, boards listen to what others have to say, they consult the experts and their stakeholders, and then say:

- Where should we be in five years' time?
- The external environment means that we have to rethink...
- This is a golden opportunity to...
- We can come out of this a stronger organisation by...
- Our pupils will leave better prepared for the next stage in their life if we...

Stretch

To challenge and improve an organisation, boards that are stretching say:

- Can't we do any better than that?
- Surely we can improve by more than 5%?
- Have you thought of doing it differently, more creatively?
- Can we create a strategic alliance for this?
- Couldn't we develop a social enterprise to do this?

Confidentiality

It is also critical that any suggestion that a member has broken confidentiality is followed up appropriately by the chair without assuming guilt. Members of the board must of course observe complete confidentiality when matters are deemed confidential or where they concern specific members of staff or pupils, both inside and outside school. They can also be expected to exercise the greatest prudence at all times when discussions regarding school business arise outside a governing board meeting, and not to reveal the details of any governing board vote. A clear breach of confidentiality cannot be overlooked and must be taken through the correct process to remove the member from the board, if the member does not resign.

3.4 The behaviours of a high-performing board

Much of the skill of governance is getting the balance right, for example, those governing boards that do best in providing strategic leadership combine a high degree of challenge with high levels of support to the headteacher and senior leadership team. The DfE's Competence Framework for Governance identifies seven Cs – attributes that those governing should possess: committed; confident; curious; challenging; collaborative; critical; and creative.

A high-performing chair wants to achieve a high-performing board that does not require the level of interventions and courageous conversations described in the previous chapter. We have already introduced the need to stay focused on the strategic, alongside the ability to generate ideas and think creatively.

Qualities of a good board

- a chair who values all perspectives and encourages open debate
- members who are able to express and listen to different views
- values facts – the whole truth and nothing but the truth – even when posing challenges
- an ability to work together for the common good even when there are difficult decisions to make
- tension is acknowledged and managed constructively to inform decisions
- mutual respect
- a welcome to new members
- a willingness to review its processes and update its habits

3.5 Reviewing governance

This needs to happen at all levels, from the chair and individual governors to the whole board. The chair should set an example. Research from other sectors has shown two areas of governance performance are generally rated less well than other aspects: one is the chair's relationship with the chief executive (we cover the relationship with the headteacher in the next chapter) and the second is the commitment of the chair to review her/his personal performance and that of other members of the board.

> " Good chairs also ask for regular feedback from their governing board to improve their own effectiveness and have an annual conversation with each governor to discuss the impact of their contribution to the work of the governing board. "

DfE Governance Handbook, October 2020

A 360-degree review of your own performance

A chair needs to review her/his own performance in order to increase awareness of strengths and weaknesses in the role, and identify areas for development. This can be done informally by asking a number of colleagues, including the headteacher and relevant partners, for feedback on your work as a chair of governors. A 360-degree review plus mentoring call can be purchased direct from NGA.

A 360° appraisal provides a unique opportunity to gain valuable insights into your leadership strengths and development needs. NGA's online appraisal tool is available for both chairs and aspiring chairs. As it is based on the DfE's Competency Framework for Governance, it provides a comprehensive snapshot of your leadership skills.

The online appraisal is simple to set up, seeks confidential feedback from your peers, and includes a mentoring session with an NGA consultant to guide you through the analysis of the report and the identification of key areas for development. Template documents to help you analyse your appraisal report and create a personal development plan are included in the package.

www.nga.org.uk/360

Research shows chairs often rate themselves higher on performance characteristics compared with how they are rated by other board members, and particularly compared with the rating by the chief executive. The results of 360-degree reviews need discussion with an experienced and impartial expert.

The review groups the competencies into three clusters:

- developing yourself to lead strategically: conceptual thinking; analytical thinking; future focus; information; integrity; personal drive; self-awareness; resilience and emotional maturity
- leading people: relating to others; holding others to account; developing others; inspiring others
- leading in the community: serving others; partnership working; broad organisational understanding; impact and influence

Appraisal of governors and trustees

Performance management of volunteers on the board in other sectors is becoming increasingly common, but is as yet still underdeveloped for school governors, despite inclusion of the 'annual conversation' for feedback in the DfE Governance Handbook for several years.

NGA thinks it is important that governing boards become more proactive in assessing and supporting individual governors' contributions. This can be done very informally with the chair – or the vice chair – having an annual meeting with each governor/trustee to discuss their contribution to the board, whether their skills are being used well, and how this might be enhanced. Views can also be sought about board dynamics and perceived effectiveness, and the performance of the chair. NGA has a template in the guidance centre with suggested topics to cover.

Feedback suggests such conversations have been working well. Governors are pleased to have their views sought and their contributions acknowledged and, if handled well, those who are perhaps better suited to other volunteering, such as listening to children read, accompanying pupils on school trips, mentoring students, or helping with extra-curricular activities, can be gently reminded that resignation is a dignified option.

Auditing board effectiveness

It is very important that the governing board reviews its performance as a whole. We recommend that this exercise is carried out internally on an annual basis and an external facilitator is considered when needed, possibly every three years.

It is the chair's role – with the clerk's help – to make sure that this happens effectively. A skills audit is one facet, but further consideration is then needed as to how these skills are used in practice and to what effect. There are a number of ways in which self-evaluation can be done:

- Against the criteria Ofsted uses to judge governance.
- By using the 20 Key Questions for the Governing Board to Ask Itself, developed by the All Party Parliamentary Group (APPG) for Governance and Leadership. These can be found at www.nga.org.uk, where NGA members can download further help on how to use the questions from our guidance centre. There is a version of 21 questions for MAT boards.
- By using an electronic board evaluation tool, for example, NGA's governing board self-review, which can be purchased from www.nga.org.uk. This tool collects the views of all governors, the clerk and senior leaders, producing a straightforward analysis. It includes a mentoring call so that the results can be fully interpreted and any issues and training needs flagged.
- By using the Governor Mark framework, which can be downloaded free, although receiving accreditation has a charge.
- By using other commercially available governor evaluation packages.
- A review by an external party such as a national leader of governance, local authority governor services, NGA's consultancy service, or another educational consultancy.

External reviews of governance

Reviewing board effectiveness is considered good practice in all sectors. NGA recommends that all governing boards externally review their performance approximately every three years, or when there are significant changes to the governance structure and/or practice of the organisation.

NGA has been carrying out external reviews of governance for over seven years and has built particular expertise in the governance of multi academy trusts. This extends to reviewing the governance of financial matters.

NGA's team of consultants are all governance experts and can undertake external reviews of governance of academy trust boards and maintained school governing bodies.

www.nga.org.uk/consultancy

❝ An external review of governance was carried out promptly following the previous inspection. The review is a model of good practice. It is detailed, precise and thorough. ❞

Ofsted report commenting on an NGA external review of governance

Self-evaluation

This is a simple-to-set-up online self-evaluation with question sets designed specifically for:

- Boards governing a single school (maintained or single academy trust)
- Federation governing bodies
- Multi academy trust boards
- Academy committees (LGBs) in MATs

All board members, senior executive leaders and the clerk complete the self-evaluation questions which populate two reports – a summary report and one which includes all respondent comments. Self-evaluating your board's effectiveness in this way not only provides the board with valuable insight into how it is working, but also provides concrete evidence that the board is taking its own performance seriously.

www.nga.org.uk/online-evaluation

 ## Developing the team: checklist

- Have all new governors/trustees been inducted well?
- Have you carried out a skills audit of your governing board? See www.nga.org.uk for a model skills audit.
- Have you got the full range of necessary skills and knowledge on the governing board? If not, recruit someone to fill a gap when the next feasible vacancy arises and provide training to others.
- Is your board diverse when it comes to age, gender, ethnicity and background?
- Do you know about the Inspiring Governance recruitment service, which provides a bank of prospective volunteers?
- Do you interview candidates (who are not elected) who wish to join the board?
- Does your clerk keep a record of training available and attendance? Have all governors been on recent appropriate training?
- Do you have a governing board development budget? Is it used?
- Do you pay governors' expenses?
- Are you acting as a model, taking up opportunities for training and development?
- Are all governors and trustees attending meetings and if not, has this been discussed?
- Do you conduct exit interviews with governors who leave before their term of office expires?
- Do you have a plan for developing other members of the team? See chapter 3.1 and chapter 7.2
- Do you have a practice of only having governors serve for up to eight years (two terms of four years)?
- Do you re-elect or re-appoint your chair and chairs of committees each year?
- Have you been in post as chair at the same school for more than six years? If so, consider it time to move on.
- If you have been chair for more than three years, are you actively recruiting or developing someone to take over?
- Have you undertaken a 360-degree review of your own performance?
- Are you undertaking appraisals of members of the governing board?
- Is your governing board having an impact?

The chair, the headteacher and accountability

4

The school's leadership team and the governing board have different but complementary roles and responsibilities for the strategic direction and the success of the school.

> " It is not just board functioning that benefits from a high-quality chair-CEO relationship, the organisation benefits also. "

Professor Chris James of the University of Bath in a literature review of the role of the chair

In maintained schools, the headteacher is usually an ex-officio governor. In some cases, when schools convert to academy status, this practice has continued and this in turn has led to some CEOs of multi academy trusts (MATs) also being trustees. NGA does not consider it to be good practice, but our stance is still a contentious issue for some CEOs. The Department for Education (DfE) has been slow to address this issue but, as a charitable company, the trust board is best comprised of non-executive trustees. In situations where executive leaders are also trustees, they are in effect marking their own homework. Executive leaders report to the board, submit papers and should be asked to attend meetings, but being trustees themselves is a clear conflict of interests.

Understanding the roles

> " The chair is the boss of the board of directors, not of the company. Many chairs do not realise this and act as if they control every aspect of the organisation. This is unwise and brings them into immediate conflict with the executives, who are responsible for the day-to-day operations of the enterprise. "

The Fish Rots from the Head: developing effective board directors by Bob Garratt

In 2019 NGA published an updated edition of What Governing Boards and School Leaders Should Expect From Each Other jointly with ASCL (Association of School and College Leaders), ISBL (Institute of School Business Leadership), NAHT (National Association of Head Teachers) and the Local Government Association. This document is available at www.nga.org.uk.

Where the respective roles are well understood, a climate of respect, cooperation and common purpose can prevail. However, not all heads approach the relationship in this manner, with some headteachers seeing the governing board as a threat or a nuisance, an obstruction to their

DfE competencies for a chair: part 3

- understands the process and documentation needed to make decisions related to leadership appraisal
- is confident and prepared in undertaking leadership appraisal
- is able to explain to the board their proposals on leadership pay awards for approval
- ensures the board holds executive leaders to account for financial and business management, as much as educational outcomes
- understands the links that the organisation needs to make with the wider community
- understands the impact and influence that a leader in the community can have, particularly on educational issues
- communicates clearly with colleagues, parents and carers, partners and other agencies, and checks that their message has been heard and understood
- considers how to tailor their communication style in order to build rapport and confidence with stakeholders

ability to lead the school. They may not have seen in practice a governing board that adds value to the work of the staff and to the pupils' outcomes.

The governance and accountability framework may, at first, be daunting in its multiplicity, complexity, and lack of clear definition. But by investing time and thought, this very framework and the key relationship with the chair should come to be seen as a protection – to both the head and the school – rather than a threat or imposition. The chair, while being aware of these sensitivities, needs to ensure the head does understand the expectations and the respective roles. Boards are unlikely to be able to play their role to the full if the lead executive does not recognise the board's centrality nor accept the responsibility of ensuring the board can function effectively.

In maintained schools, the regulations set out in black and white that the "headteacher is accountable to the governing body for the performance of all his or her responsibilities and... must comply with any reasonable request from the governing body". While this should not be used as a stick to beat headteachers with, it can be a powerful aid when dealing with recalcitrant headteachers. An academy trust's articles of association tend to deal with it slightly differently: "the business of the Academy Trust shall be managed by the Trustees, who may exercise all the powers of the Academy Trust... In the exercise of their powers and functions, the Trustees may consider any advice given by the [Chief Executive Officer]/[Principal]".

An effective chair has to:

- understand that the headteacher is not a mere agent of the board, but a strategic leader as well as a manager, while ensuring the headteacher understands her/his own accountability to the board

- work in partnership with the headteacher, developing a professional relationship by providing regular contact, appropriate support, encouragement and challenge

- ensure all governors concentrate on their strategic role, receive information fit for purpose and hold the headteacher to account, without interfering in the executive role

- where required, represent the governing board in its dealings with external parties and be an advocate for the school

- ensure the governing board has set a performance management policy and culture that drives continuing professional development (CPD) and school improvement

- ensure the governing board is equipped to recruit senior leaders and that the headteacher is equipped to recruit other staff

Alongside the relationship of the executive management – or as we term them in schools, rather confusingly, the school leadership – with the governing board, there is also the relationship of the two individual leaders – the headteacher (or chief executive) and the chair. This is perhaps the most important relationship in the school, and should be negotiated on the understanding that the chair leads the governing board and the headteacher (or chief executive) leads and manages the school(s). It is rather overlooked in the DfE's competencies for chairs.

A governing board will expect the chair to both support and challenge the headteacher in order to make sure school leadership and management is strong, as well as strengthening governance by ensuring the board is provided with the information it needs to do its job well by the headteacher. It has been reported to NGA that during COVID-19 the relationships between heads and their boards strengthened.

It is plainly very desirable that the head should enjoy the governing board's support, and the chair plays an important part in this. Heads are entitled to look to the chair for dispassionate advice; for encouragement when things are difficult; for praise for their efforts and successes; and for a frank but constructive discussion if they perform less than well. The chair is the governor who sees the head most often, both formally and informally, and is well placed to give a view – asked for or not – on how the governing board sees its responsibilities; on which matters governors might wish to be informed, advised or consulted; and what views they might hold on particular issues. This process is likely to be more intensive and time-consuming for chairs in particular instances, such as schools with low pupil performance or with a new first-time head. When the relationship between the chair and the head is working at its best, it can provide inspiration as well as support to the headteacher.

It is the responsibility of both the chair and headteacher to establish and foster a professional relationship based on trust and mutual respect. It is essential that the chair and the head agree about the need for effective challenge as well as support, and for an open dialogue about the strengths and weaknesses of the school. As well as an understanding of the roles, the relationship between chair and headteacher benefits from:

- a shared vision and sense of common purpose; a joint endeavour

- good communication, with a clear understanding of each other's preferences regarding communication style and format

- reflection on and time spent understanding each other's personality, motivations and position, and developing the relationship
- development opportunities for both, together and separately
- knowing that they can get support for their partnership through services like facilitation and mediation if it proves necessary

The relationship is a multifaceted one, as the chair leads the body that not only sets the vision, ethos and strategic direction of the school, but also hires, performance manages and can fire the headteacher who is tasked with delivering the vision. This can be difficult to navigate, but it is not exclusive to schools. In all sectors, it is recognised that the board chair and the chief executive should provide a check and balance for each other's authority. Challenging each other within safe boundaries is the norm. There should be an expressed understanding that the chair and the headteacher can be confidential sounding boards for each other, and within that confidentiality can deal with (and forgive) the mistakes that both will inevitably make.
In spite of the formal hierarchical structure that makes the headteacher accountable to the board, the day-to-day reality is that the headteacher will be seen as the face of the leadership by pupils, parents and staff. Some tasks may be worked on together, such as design of the school's strategy or a communications plan for a major event, which will benefit from early discussion between the headteacher and the chair.

School leaders should not be micromanaged, and it is part of the chair's role to ensure that the governing board understands the difference between strategic and operational decision-making. Managerial and operational decisions should be left to the headteacher and her/his staff (see chapter 1.2). Yet, with the exception of some MATs and federations, the chair is the closest that the headteacher has to a line manager (although we do not tend to use this language); the difference being that a well-paid professional should not need the same level of supervision as other employees.

However, in effect, the regular contact between a chair and a head is in part playing that role, and in addition governors both undertake the head's appraisal and agree on pay rises. There may also be times when a headteacher is struggling with the job and the chair will find her/himself very much involved in ensuring support for the professional leader, but also having to make a difficult decision as to how and when to share information with the rest of the governing board, and how much information to share.

4.1 Negotiating the working relationship

Any working relationship has to be negotiated between the two individuals with a mutual understanding of the expectations on both parties. For an effective relationship to develop between the chair and the head, there must be an agreed understanding of the roles and responsibilities, thus making sure no opportunity for confusion arises. The governing board's more specific duties are laid down in regulations for maintained schools and in articles of association for academies. The role of local governing bodies in a MAT should be set down in a scheme of delegation (SoD). The chair and the head need to be familiar with both the articles and the SoD.

> " With a volunteer board overseeing the work of a professional chief executive and constrained by the difficulty of agreeing appropriate performance measures, the relationship between the board and the chief executive is more subtle than in for-profit or public sector organisations. "
>
> David Fishel, Boards That Work: a guide for charity trustees

Key issues to address in building a professional relationship with the head

- mission: a shared understanding of the organisation's purpose and strategic priorities
- ethical leadership: a shared understanding of the Nolan principles and virtues
- roles: defined and respected, with the emphasis on preventing overlaps and territorial disputes
- expectations on behaviours: discussed and understood
- mature communication: dispassionate and high-quality communication is essential
- no surprises: should ensure each other is aware of any important and relevant developments
- public unity: chair and head should present a united public front on issues of fundamental importance
- mutual support, challenge and advice: be willing to act as confidential 'sounding boards'
- mutual care, trust and respect: giving credit and thanks with a generosity of spirit to each other and all involved in the shared enterprise

The context in which negotiation takes place will also affect both the way in which it is negotiated and the outcome of the negotiation. The notion of the hierarchy with the board being the headteacher's 'boss' is not language commonly used, and it is not an expression NGA would encourage a chair to use, except in extremis. However, it is perfectly reasonable to remind a senior executive leader that they are an employee. This confusion of role has been compounded in some academy trusts where founder CEOs have been appointed as trustees, thus effectively becoming their own boss. This is not good practice and chairs of trust boards should bring this to the attention of the board and seek change if this is the case.

> Governing boards are the strategic decision-makers and vision-setters in every school and academy. They play a vital role in ensuring the best possible education for every child by creating robust accountability for executive leaders.

Lord Nash, parliamentary under secretary of state for schools with particular responsibility for governance, in his foreword to the DfE Governance Handbook

Compared with other sectors, heads can sometimes be reluctant to accept the authority of the governing board and the importance of the role of the chair. That is not to say it is simple in other sectors; comparative research shows that there can be ambiguity and conflict between the board chair and chief executive role in all settings, and that chairs of trustees and chief executives of voluntary organisations found sorting out the allocation of responsibility and authority particularly problematic. It was concluded that as board chairs in voluntary organisations have limited time and little formal authority, much therefore depends on the quality of the board chair-CEO relationship.

Some heads have difficulty in accepting someone from outside the education profession being not only in a leadership role in a school, but also the lead influence in determining the expert's career progression and remuneration. This approach is the norm in some other sectors, with chief executives being held to account by non-executives, and in some other jurisdictions such as schools in the United States, where democratically elected community school boards hire, performance manage and fire.

However, the school sector in England can be very internally focused; there can be an arrogance displayed in dismissing the knowledge and wisdom that governors, trustees and the chair may bring from their own employment or life experiences (the majority of chairs of governing boards are themselves professional people). On the other hand, good heads acknowledge – and welcome – the increasing

focus on accountability through good school governance by investing in developing an effective relationship with the chair. This in turn shows the world – and Ofsted – that the organisation is doing its job well. Indeed, recent research showed the majority of headteachers do work hard at the relationship with the chair. However, board observations often still show behaviours of chief executives that suggest that they may not have understood the nature of their relationship with the board of trustees.

During the appointment process, a prospective head may talk to governors about building sound relationships, only to get into the job and, amid the numerous other duties and initiatives, fail to invest time or thought in properly developing such relationships. This may manifest itself in a range of behaviours, for example, speaking at length and dominating board meetings; not having papers ready for distribution in advance of meetings; failing to provide the requested information in the appropriate format; dismissing or failing to act on governing board suggestions; sidelining the chair; swamping the chair or board in detail; wasting time by pointing the way down blind alleys or involving the governing board in pro-bono activities rather than its core functions. A good chair will seek to address such issues, but bear in mind this is likely to be one of those 'courageous conversations'.

The arrival of a new head or new chair necessitates an open, but confidential, professional discussion about what each expects of the other. This should include the means of future communication, including how often they will talk or meet. You should also seek to clarify with each other, and the clerk, the custom and practice of the governing board's business (see chapter 6.3). Establishing an open and honest dialogue very early on will make it much easier for the chair and the head to discuss whether the governance arrangements, and the whole myriad of related processes (for example, the headteacher's performance management, school evaluation cycle, financial reporting), are acceptable to both parties and if not, how to move towards a different and more effective approach. As the lead professional, the head can easily access the information, advice and guidance that can be used in conjunction with the experience of the chair to move governance forward and ensure effective accountability.

In addition, it is critical to reach agreement on that which is strategic and that which is operational, and on what information, in what format and on what issues (including, for example, the quality of teaching, pupil progress, staff performance management) is required. The head must be prepared to be questioned on this information, to facilitate the gathering of any external advice requested by the governing board, and to initiate and respond to other information-gathering exercises requested by the board (such as parental surveys or student focus groups). As well as monitoring reports, there will be other papers containing proposals that need to be circulated to board members at least a week in advance of meetings. The chair may often discuss the contents at an early stage and even comment on the draft paper, especially if the senior leaders are not experienced in writing focused strategic papers containing options, risk assessments and possibly costings.

It is arguable how much of a role the head has in ensuring the development of the governing board; s/he should certainly address any issues that arise with the chair but not trespass on the chair's role of developing the team.

The head can use her/his professionalism to address governance training needs (for her/himself, staff and governors), to enable prompt payment of expenses and by being open about succession planning (for both the staff and the governing board).

Training for heads and aspiring heads, such as the National Professional Qualification for Headship (NPQH), has tended to devote very little time to how the head can and should work with her/his governing board, but we have lobbied for this to change in future. Many first-time heads are uncertain about what is expected from them, for example, in terms of reporting to the governing board, and practice is known to be very varied. NGA and Inspiring Governance have been

The chair-headteacher relationship

An excerpt from an article in Governing Matters, NGA's membership magazine Jan/Feb 2013 by Professor Chris James of the University of Bath

Our research confirmed that the chair-headteacher relationship is generally important to both parties. By and large, they had similar views of the relationship although there were some differences. For example, heads accepted that chairs should challenge them; chairs did not agree so wholeheartedly that the heads saw it that way. Headteachers felt they were open with chairs; chairs did not always agree with them on that.

The relationship was often characterised as 'professional' and had two particular aspects. There was a 'bond', although typically chairs and headteachers were not friends, and the relationship enabled mutual sensemaking.

They used each other as sounding boards to make sense of issues. The relationship developed over time and was a two-way interaction; the chairs and the headteachers influenced each other. Headteachers found it difficult working with underperforming chairs, and chairs struggled when working with underperforming heads.

Managing the average performer was thus problematic for both heads and chairs. Meetings and contact were very important, as was the chair's availability. It was a private relationship (things may be said in the privacy of the headteacher's office, for example, that would not be said in public). There was also a public aspect to the relationship where differences of view might be temporarily put aside. Both chairs and heads felt they worked at the relationship and endeavoured to make it function properly. The headteachers and the chairs we interviewed varied considerably in age, gender, ethnicity and experience.

There was no magic combination of particular features. … From a statistical analysis of the survey data, we were

able to reach the following conclusions about the chair-headteacher relationship:

- Relationship quality does not correlate with school type, size, socio-economic context or pupil performance. The relationship can work well in any setting.

- Relationship quality is better if the chair is retired or gets paid time off work for governing. This suggests that the chair being available and accessible is important, as is being able to make the relationship a priority.

- A poor relationship correlates strongly with poor governing board functioning, which points to the importance of the relationship for governing generally.

What makes the relationship work?

The research revealed a number of qualities that make the relationship work:

- mutuality – they learned from and interacted on an equal footing

- complementarity – their qualities and capabilities complemented each other

- honesty and openness

- trust and respect

- commitment – to the role and the success of the school

- capability – in their respective positions

Professor James reporting on Chris James et al (2013).
The chair of the school governing body in England: roles, relationships, and responsibilities.

promoting the practice of middle leaders volunteering as governors in other schools, usually in a different phase, as good CPD: www.nga.org.uk/Educators-on-Board.

Communication with the head

Before COVID-19 most chairs and heads found it worked best for them to have regular, diarised meetings in school. Others keep in touch on a more ad-hoc basis, meeting face-to-face only when necessary and using phone and email contact in between times. It is important that the chair and the headteacher find mutually convenient arrangements that do not take up too much time, given both parties' commitments. Just as a good chair takes note of the head's work/life balance, a good head should give consideration to the chair's other commitments. Good chairs value and thank professional school leaders and it is reasonable to expect that the paid professional should acknowledge the work of the volunteer body and, in particular, the chair.

The chair's relationship with the head, and their amount of contact, will differ depending on time commitments; the size and phase of the school; the issues to be discussed; the skills and experience of both parties; and the personalities and preferences of those involved. It is likely that the frequency of contact will be greater where there is a newly appointed head or a new chair. There is no blueprint, but a regular pattern is desirable. Some chairs meet the headteacher weekly; however, an experienced chair performing a strategic function should not need to do this. Unless there are exceptional challenges at the school, monthly face-to-face meetings with the head will usually be more appropriate and effective, especially if the head is also experienced.

A chair may want to visit more often to be visible in school, for example, to staff, but simply to be visible is not a sufficient reason. Some chairs do drop in to school fairly frequently and can be defensive when challenged about this practice. If this has become a habit, it needs to be reviewed honestly with the headteacher. Some headteachers welcome this attention, but if it is not entirely clear why the chair of the board needs to visit on any particular occasion, this should be raised and discussed.

The chair and the head need to be able to contact each other in an emergency, but each must also respect the other's privacy and work/life balance. It is good practice for the chair to offer a full range of contact details to the head and vice versa, but neither party can expect immediate accessibility. The chair should keep the head informed about periods of holiday and/or absence; during these periods the vice chair should step in to cover the chair's duties, with the full knowledge of the governing board.

New chairs of maintained schools also need to be aware that local authorities frequently send information to the school addressed to "The headteacher and chair of governors"; it is useful to agree early in the relationship just how the chair will receive their copy of such information.

The DfE also tends to ask heads to ensure chairs get copies of relevant information. Too often, a school office will ensure that the head gets her/his copy, and completely forget about sending a copy to the chair.

There are potential problems in the free and frank exchange of views between the head and the chair. There are some things that it is important for the head to be able to discuss informally with the chair, which may at a later date be the subject of formal proceedings before the governing board or a committee of governors, for example, issues of discipline, grievance or any complaint involving a member of staff. Informal conversations between the chair and the head on such matters need to remain confidential.

Members of the governing board should not feel that sides have been taken or decisions made behind their backs, so careful thought must be given to what information should be confidential to the head and the chair, and what should properly be shared with the governing board. It is vital that other governors understand that there will be matters discussed between the head and the chair that must remain between the two of them. Most of these matters will relate to individual employees or pupils. All governing boards must have a disciplinary and/or appeals committee, which may meet from time to time to hear such cases. Where the chair has been involved in any early discussions of the matter, s/he should not take part in the subsequent formal proceedings. Another governor – possibly the vice chair – will have to chair any formal hearing.

It can sometimes be tempting for the head and chair to sort things out on their own; however, chairs must resist the temptation to make decisions outside the framework agreed by the governing board. A chair is only able to make decisions when a matter is urgent (see chapter 6.6).

Good communication is the key to avoiding embarrassment and misunderstandings; there should be no public surprises. An easy way for relationships between the chair and the head to deteriorate is if items are introduced at the governing board meeting that take the other by surprise. The chair is best placed to have early informal conversations with the head about any issues of concern about the head's performance, but these need to be handled sensitively, and in advance of formal performance management arrangements (see chapter 4.7).

A mature relationship

Experience and research from a range of sectors show that shared values and personal compatibility are important in making this relationship work. Personal compatibility does not mean similar, but with synergy. Even where both the chair and the headteacher are extremely committed to the ethos and mission of the school, they may differ on the direction, policy or tactics of achieving their shared vision. Thought has to be given to when the pair need to present a united front (in public) and when expressing disagreements within a board meeting is necessary. Even though the chair acting as a confidential sounding board can be important, this must not prevent issues being referred to the whole board when appropriate.

Neither party should dominate and each must respect what the other brings. A generosity of spirit towards the headteacher is helpful as they are likely to be spending a significant part of their life delivering the organisation's mission. Challenge is most productive in an atmosphere of trust, which in turn is fundamental to a good relationship. How that relationship develops will depend on the couple's temperaments and the style of challenge may vary; energetic challenge may be welcomed by many headteachers while others may react better to a more reflective and measured approach. Research from the USA in 2008 showed that the more diverse the interactions between chairs and CEO the better the trust developed, but the quality of the interactions mattered more than the quantity.

In time, one would expect the relationship to be close but not personal, and certainly not cosy or exclusive. Too much similarity of thought can be dangerous, leading to blind spots, complacency and the inability to identify risk. Independence of thought is important, and the headteacher should understand when the chair needs to seek another opinion or source of information. For a lot of the time a chair will be helicoptering above the work of the headteacher, but there are occasions when it is perfectly valid for them to want to delve more deeply into an area of potential concern in order to satisfy themselves that there is no risk or alternative explanation.

A difficult relationship

Relationships can of course be made difficult by either party, or both, especially where they have a different outlook or a misunderstanding about their respective roles. Headteachers may require training on governance, just as much as new governors or chairs. As long as the pair are not entirely incompatible, different personal approaches can be made into an asset. This relationship is not a friendship, but a professional relationship that can gain from both people's attitudes, approaches and experiences, as long as there is honesty and respect.

A report on the relationship between chair and lead executives within the NHS identified three areas of potential problems:

- clashes of personality
- conflict caused by the lack of clarity of the roles (eg chairs micromanaging)
- constraints on the time or energy of the chair, which could lead to the conflict becoming unresolved

However, it has been shown in other sectors where there are similar tensions between pairings, such as the financial sector, that the deficiencies in the relationship are primarily related to patterns of behaviour.

Some headteachers and CEOs disempower their governing board, deliberately or unknowingly, in a number of different ways – through the manner in which they conduct themselves or by the type of information provided to the meetings. S/he may delay major decisions until they are urgent; raise them under AOB without written papers; fill the board agenda with minor issues, sometimes even operational ones; flood the board with unnecessary detail; or fail to act on the decisions of the board. This behaviour could have developed if a previous chair had been too weak and lacking in the ability to challenge it.

The chair will need to tackle these issues directly and make sure governors receive high-quality board papers that are succinct and to the point, concentrate on governance issues and arrive in good time. Headteachers may seek out – or even put forward – governors as allies, especially those who do not like to challenge the professional leaders.

This can be time-consuming for the chair to rectify at one-to-one meetings and it may be that performance appraisal needs to be used to improve the situation and for the headteacher to understand its seriousness.

All-powerful chief executives can also be seen in other sectors; the parliamentary report into Kids Company gave evidence to show "how unaccountable and dominant trustees had allowed her [the chief executive] to become, and how far she was able to insist on maintaining personal control". This was compounded in that the chief executive was also the founder of the charity. In the schools sector we need to aware of the risk of 'founder syndrome' in free schools and those MATs set up by the individual who is now the lead executive.

4.2 The chair's external role

The chair is the obvious person to represent the governing board on the occasions when a spokesperson is necessary or desirable. This is certainly the case when the governing board needs to address parents or the staff group. However, there will also be times when the chair is properly called on to address external audiences, but s/he should not be overburdened with this responsibility except when it is vital that the governing board is seen as accountable.

A new chair should give thought to how this role is managed, given her/his own skills and time constraints and those of the vice chair, and discuss it with the headteacher. For example, a chair may be used more often as an external spokesperson for the school where their skills or experience in this area are more extensive than the head's. Representing the school can be shared as long as there is agreement on how, why and when this will happen.

Some chairs report that being the external 'face' of the school is one of the most fulfilling and enjoyable aspects of the role, but it is important that this is kept in proportion and does not step on the toes of the headteacher. The senior leadership team should be capable of representing and promoting the school in the usual run of things. Headteachers in particular are expected to be the face of the school with parents and the local community.

However, there are occasions when it may be necessary for the chair of the accountable body of a school, federation or trust to support the senior leadership or to make a public statement. This could be when the press becomes interested in the school, for example, if the school has been rated as 'inadequate' by Ofsted; there had been an accident or a violent incident; a school trip has ended in disaster; an adult is suspected of child abuse; or a headteacher or bursar is accused of embezzlement or other misconduct. On the other hand, a chair should not feel obliged to respond to every press enquiry: no comment may be the best option. The chair may want to seek external advice and expertise in a time of crisis, for example, from the local authority in a maintained school.

The chair may be needed to represent the school at external meetings with partners, the local authority, the diocese or the DfE. Often this will be alongside the headteacher/CEO. NGA believes it is good practice for chairs and headteachers to attend discussions about the future direction of the school/trust or its possible structure together (see chapter 5.5 for meetings with Ofsted). Chairs of academy committees will be involved in meetings with trustees or the lead executives of MATs, but these should not be viewed as external meetings.

Other members of the governing board will come from local organisations, including employers, bringing a useful perspective and potentially another route for engagement with the local community. The chair does not need to undertake this liaison, but needs to know that a range of useful links have been made. If significant issues are affecting the school's standing in the local community, the chair or another governor may need to be involved in any meeting with local residents, businesses or other organisations as an ambassador for the school/trust. Alternatively, the chair may feel the head or another senior leader is best placed to represent the school and the contact can be handed to them.

4.3 Recruiting a headteacher

The appointment of the school's next headteacher or the senior executive of the MAT can be the most significant action a governing board undertakes. There is much documentation available to inform and advise governing boards on how to go about the identification and appointment of a suitable person at www.nga.org.uk/Knowledge-Centre as well as a Learning Link module.

In maintained schools, it is the chair's role to ensure the local authority is informed of the outgoing head's decision to leave. In MATs, the central staff will take over and support the recruitment process, and usually decide the panel that will undertake the recruitment; we would expect this to include at least the chair of the academy committee. Otherwise the chair will find her/himself having a pivotal role in leading the recruitment process, which is a major commitment. S/he must have access to human resources (HR) advice and liaise with all parties, including the foundation or diocese if relevant.

The chair should ensure the governing board takes the opportunity to consider whether replacing the departing headteacher with the same role is the best option for the school. These discussions can be had before notice is given, and often should be as part of succession planning. Unfortunately, some governing boards do not consider federation or other organisational changes, such as joining a MAT, that may offer different benefits to the school over time until the point of the head's resignation.

There may be internal and external views about any possible changes, which the chair and governors will need to consider while coming to their own view. An interim solution must be found if an initial recruitment is unsuccessful or if time is needed to explore the possibility of an executive principal who has responsibility for two schools. MATs and federations are more likely to be able to make these decisions quickly and may have leaders to deploy from elsewhere within the group of schools.

Research NGA carried out with Future Leaders and the National Foundation for Educational Research (NFER), Executive Headteachers: what's in a name? confirmed that when governing boards are changing the senior executive roles, they are not always clear about the nature of the role nor do they always recruit in an objective fashion with a job description and a person specification. Although this may have been improving since the research, there are still job descriptions and recruitment processes that are inadequate in some MATs where senior leadership posts are evolving.

The chair can help this process by:

- supporting succession planning and leadership development among the staff, and particularly within the leadership team, as preparation for headship either at your school or elsewhere

- ensuring sound planning to see the school through the change, especially if an unforeseen circumstance arises and there is the danger of a gap in the leadership

- ensuring that the governing board has the opportunity to review and confirm or revise the school's vision, and that this is clearly articulated

- ensuring that the governing board is aware of the headteacher national standards

- ensuring that there is a clear job description for every senior role and that these complement each other and between them cover all the required responsibilities

- ensuring that governors have experience and confidence in assessing and appointing (some governors may have experience from their own professional lives while others will need to be encouraged to attend training sessions)

- ensuring that the governing board understands the way in which it can determine the headteacher's pay (and if a maintained school, is aware of the national pay scale and the discretions within those rules) and seeks out benchmarks

- working with the clerk to ensure that the necessary additional meetings are well planned and have all the necessary paperwork and housekeeping arrangements in place

Induction

It is important that the new headteacher has an appropriate induction programme, and the chair has a role in ensuring this is planned and happens. Headteachers, particularly those new to the role, should be offered a mentor, usually another more experienced, successful headteacher. The professional development of the headteacher is sometimes overlooked, even at this early stage. The chair should have a conversation about what areas of the role are likely to be the most challenging. NGA's Annual Governance Survey shows that organisational management, especially finance and HR, parental complaints, and embedding culture and

strategy often show up gaps in a new head's knowledge. It may be that some heads of school within MATs do not have responsibility for some functions that are now overseen centrally, such as budgeting and premises.

Many headteachers appreciate the offer of coaching. This is no reflection on shortcomings in the relationship between the chair and the headteacher. A trained coach, especially one with an education background, performs a supplementary role.

4.4 Performance management

Once appointed, effective oversight of the headteacher's or chief executive's performance is arguably the most important ongoing role for the governing board. However, this is unlikely to be a role retained fully by an academy committee of a MAT, as the senior executives are being paid to line manage the headteachers.

The governing body in a maintained school has a legal duty to ensure that effective performance management, including annual appraisal, is carried out for the teaching staff and headteacher. The headteacher is directly responsible for the performance appraisal of the teaching staff, as well as all other staff, and the governing body is directly responsible for the performance appraisal of the head. There are no formal legal requirements on academies in relation to performance management, but it is good practice to have a policy and procedures in place. Academies are subject to the same Ofsted inspection regime as other schools, which requires evidence of appraisal systems and their effect on school standards.

The appraisal of the headteacher (or the chief executive of a MAT), with its setting and reviewing of objectives, is a very important lever for the governing board in influencing the performance of the organisation and the outcomes for pupils. However, where you are governing a school in a MAT, the annual appraisal of the headteacher is most likely to fall to an executive headteacher or the chief executive, although the chair of the academy committee will usually be asked to contribute to the process and attend the meeting. This should be covered by the MAT's SoD. The chair should request input.

It is good practice for the governing board to appoint two or three governors, including the chair, to undertake the annual appraisal of the headteacher's performance. NGA thinks that it is important for the chair to be involved in the appraisal, including the conversation with any external adviser. The chair is the governor who has most contact with the headteacher throughout the year and can add information or correct any misunderstanding other reviewers may have.

NGA Headteacher/CEO performance management

NGA's team of expert governance consultants are uniquely qualified to support your governing board through the annual appraisal and performance management process.

www.nga.org.uk/consultancy

It also equates with most other situations where appraisal is undertaken by an employee's line manager. Another governor – for example, the vice chair – can be the governor to whom the head would appeal if s/he were unhappy with any aspect of the process. It is also helpful if a new member is brought into the review team each year, both to act as a fresh pair of eyes and to rotate the task among different governors so that more members of the board can contribute and test that this is a robust process.

Governing bodies of maintained schools must appoint an external adviser for the headteacher's appraisal, and it is important that this is a governing body decision, not a headteacher recommendation. Although there is no legal requirement for an external adviser for academies, trustees may want to consider this practice. However, as you would expect trustees to be experienced in performance management in their own professional lives and to have a good understanding of the school's priorities and performance, there may be no need for this. In other charitable trusts the appraisal of the chief executive may be carried out by the chair of the board alone, but NGA suggests that the practice from the school sector of having two or even three trustees is better. It prevents the relationship between the chair and the chief executive becoming too exclusive and possibly cosy.

A headteacher's performance will be measured against agreed objectives. These will usually correspond to the priorities set in the school strategy, although there should be an additional objective that relates to the headteacher's development. Development and CPD opportunities are an important aspect of the six monthly conversations, which should also cover the leader's well-being.

The regulations for maintained schools require a governing body to assess the headteacher's performance against the teacher standards and it may also use the national headteacher standards.

A strong conclusion from a DfE-funded study published in 2014 was that effective headteacher performance management (HTPM) depends on mutual respect and trust in the relationship between the governing board and the headteacher. Most frequently mentioned were openness; honesty; and the ability to be frank, to challenge and to accept challenge, with neither governors nor headteachers "afraid to say what they think". Some reported previously ineffective approaches to HTPM had been characterised by a "too-cosy relationship" between the chair, external adviser and headteacher, or a chair or external adviser unwilling to challenge the headteacher.

NGA's guidance on HTPM can be downloaded from www.nga.org.uk/performance-management.

4.5 Headteacher and executive pay

The board should ensure that a separate pay committee exists to monitor pay against performance and to ensure that any decisions relating to pay increases are not made solely by the chair or the panel who conducted the HTPM review. A pay committee should have its own terms of reference and minutes that are recorded by the clerk.

In maintained schools, the School Teachers' Pay and Conditions Document (STPCD) and leadership pay scales must be used in accordance with the school's own pay policy. These national pay scales are reviewed annually. In academy trusts, trustees should ensure that they adopt a robust pay policy after benchmarking against similar external roles in the public sector.

NGA has been concerned about exceptionally high salaries paid to a few executives for some time so we were pleased when the secretary of state said at our 2018 summer conference: "Pay needs to be proportionate, and I am clear that pay rises for non-teaching management should not exceed those awarded to teaching staff. And when considering what's fair, trusts and boards should not just compare pay rises over a single year, but look and compare over a number of years, at a time when public finances have been really stretched. This is public money and, frankly, I think that for a headteacher or chief executive to be paid more than the prime minister, this should be only in exceptional circumstances for exceptional leadership. So I want to urge all trusts to take a lead here and bear down on excessive salaries – you have our backing on that… We will be requiring academy accounts returns to detail all staff paid over £100,000 and the percentage of teaching time those individuals undertake. And, rest assured, where salaries are too high – we will publicly challenge trusts and boards to justify themselves."

The Academies Financial Handbook produced by the Education and Skills Funding Agency (ESFA) is clear on the robust procedures that need to be followed when setting executive pay, and the DfE has continued to challenge chairs of trusts that are paying high amounts to executives. This includes single academy trusts as well as MATs. NGA has produced guidance on setting executive pay that is recommended by the Association of School and College Leaders: www.nga.org.uk/executive-pay.

4.6 Professional development of the headteacher

The chair needs to ensure that the headteacher is able to develop through a variety of different means tailored to their needs and the school's. There are many opportunities available to school leaders but the conversation needs to be had, both as part of the formal appraisal and also during the regular catch-up discussions. Headteachers should be aware of the options available, but if a chair finds this is not the case, more research needs to be undertaken by other parties. This must not be squeezed out by day-to-day concerns.

Research by NFER has shown that each year approximately 10% of headteachers under normal retirement age leave headship in the state school system in England, as well as another 5% moving between schools. While it may well be inevitable, and indeed positive, that a headteacher wishes to move on to a new challenge, it is important not to make it more likely that they leave the profession by failing to support them.

The chair is responsible for ensuring a new head is inducted well, especially one in their first headship. New heads should be expected to find a mentor. A coach can be useful at any point in a career, and all heads should be encouraged to have one. Evaluation has shown that coaching has been identified by leaders as transformational, for example, helping them to be explicit about what success looks like. The chair also needs to make sure that the headteacher has access to professional networks that provide support, information, benchmarking and ideas. This should be an ongoing topic of conversation between them: how is the headteacher working with others outside the school and what are they learning from it?

In turn, the headteacher is responsible for developing the rest of the staff, in particular the senior and middle leaders, who in turn will be working to develop teachers. Their ability to do this will be central to their success in improving the school. Research has shown that supporting teachers' development

has more impact on improving pupils' outcomes than any other leadership activity. For teachers interested in taking a leadership role, Leadership Matters by Andy Buck is a good place for a school leader to begin.

Discussions of staff professional development do not usually get the time at a board meeting they deserve given the importance to school improvement. Conversations after staff appraisal in practice more often concern pay (the fiduciary) rather than investment and impact of staff development (the strategic). The chair should ensure the latter appears on the agenda.

4.7 Underperformance by the headteacher

The appraisal process may identify issues about the head's performance, or even about the head's capability for the post. Alternatively, concerns may be raised by an external body such as the local authority, a regional schools commissioner (RSC) or by Ofsted. However, it is most likely (unless a governing board is asleep on the job) that some of its members are aware of issues at a much earlier stage. It may also happen that, either because of the regular catch-ups or as a result of informal information, perhaps from parents or from another governor, the person who first becomes uneasy is the chair.

Even in the earliest stages, the chair will most probably need to have a confidential conversation with the vice chair as a sounding board. Depending on the seriousness of the concerns, they may then think it necessary to seek advice regarding the performance of the head. The first port of call may be the external adviser used for appraisal, or the senior executive in a MAT. For a maintained school, if the situation is of serious concern it would usually be discussed with the local authority. Should legal advice be necessary, the chair must contact the HR legal adviser who will have been contracted by the school (except where chairing an academy committee when this would usually be the job of an executive). If the chair of an academy committee is unsure of the process or the actions being taken by the executives, s/he should raise the issue with the chair of the MAT board.

Concerns raised by the governing board

Governors may have concerns about the performance of the headteacher arising from:

- a pattern of complaints from pupils, parents, staff or others
- the headteacher's failure to follow the strategic direction set by the governing board
- the headteacher's failure to report properly to the governing board

- the headteacher's failure to make progress on issues after a poor Ofsted judgment
- poor or deteriorating performance in national curriculum tests or public exams
- other evidence of continuing and systemic weakness in the management of the school or in its financial controls
- evidence of poor professional or personal conduct that may bring the school into disrepute

It is important that these issues are raised in a way that stresses the governing board's wish to assist the headteacher to work to improve the situation. The chair has a key role in this process, because the chair should raise any concerns informally with the head at their regular meetings before any formal process begins. Notes of those discussions should be kept. However, if informal discussions fail to achieve any improvement, prompt action will be necessary. A written report setting out the governing board's concerns should be delivered to the headteacher, with a clear timetable for improvement. This written report should make clear that failure to make sufficient progress on the matters identified in the report could result in future action following policies and procedures adopted by the governing board.

It is important that the whole governing board is not involved at this stage to ensure there are 'untainted' governors should the issue come to a grievance or disciplinary action. At this point the chair is strongly advised to seek advice from experts in employment law and practice. Each school should have an appointed HR and legal service provider. In maintained schools, this may be provided by the local authority, some of which have a very good record in supporting governing bodies with prompt and relevant advice. Others do not, and the governing body should be prepared to seek independent advice if necessary. NGA's advice service is available to GOLD members.

Dealing with allegations of misconduct

The chair will almost certainly be the first port of call for dealing with allegations of serious professional misconduct by the headteacher – these are allegations that, if true, would lead to disciplinary action and potential dismissal. In such cases, the chair may be called upon to suspend the headteacher until such time as an investigation by an independent person has taken place.

In a maintained school, the power to suspend does not rest legally with the chair, but with the governing body. However, in practice such actions nearly always fall to the chair under chair's action (see chapter 6.6), both because it may be

necessary to take action very quickly, and also to prevent other members of the governing body being 'tainted' should a governor disciplinary panel be necessary. At such times, it is essential that the chair takes appropriate professional advice from the school's HR or legal adviser. In particular, the chair needs to satisfy her/himself that there is sufficient credible evidence to warrant a suspension. It is wise to seek the advice and support of another experienced governor, most probably the vice chair. This has an added benefit as during such, admittedly relatively rare, occasions the position of chair can feel extremely onerous and lonely.

In academies, although the board of trustees as the employer of the staff has the legal responsibility, the responsibility for decisions about whether to suspend can be delegated. It should be noted that in most academy articles of association there is no specified right to take chair's action. This would need to be set out in the SoD. In most MATs disciplinary and capability processes are delegated to the executive leadership and the chair of the academy committee may need to provide evidence, but will not be responsible for leading the process.

The governing board needs to be informed why the headteacher has been suspended in broad terms (for example, while allegations of financial impropriety are investigated). However, the chair, and usually the vice chair, will be party to information that the majority of the other board members will not have seen. In effective governing boards, members will have the background and experience to understand that this is the correct procedure in such sensitive matters, but the chair nonetheless can feel isolated and friendless, especially as s/he is likely to be asked questions from all directions – staff and parents – that s/he is unlikely to be able to answer substantively. This is where a good relationship with the vice chair who can act as a confidant is invaluable.

Beyond an initial fact-finding assessment to establish the credibility of any allegations, the chair should not undertake any investigatory work; good practice dictates that an independent person is appointed to do so. Once a report into the allegations is received, the chair will need to decide whether it is necessary to set up a disciplinary panel. If the chair feels too close to the issue to decide this individually, it may be necessary to set up an initial panel to decide whether the report warrants a disciplinary hearing, and a second to conduct the hearing if this is the agreed route. The chair and any other governor who has become party to the details must not sit on any disciplinary panel.

Concerns raised by a local authority about maintained schools

An informal process involving first the head and then the chair should precede any formal complaint by the local authority. To raise a concern formally, the local authority must notify the chair. Local authorities may legitimately raise concerns with the governing bodies of maintained schools in the following circumstances:

- failure to produce an effective action plan after an Ofsted judgment of 'serious weaknesses' or 'special measures'
- poor or deteriorating performance in national curriculum tests or public exams where the worsening situation can be attributed to the head's action or inaction
- a pattern of complaints from parents, staff or governors
- evidence of continuing and systemic weakness in the management of the school or in its financial controls, which, if not tackled, risks significant disruption to the school's continuing operation

Once a written complaint is received by the chair, the head should have an opportunity to make representations to the chair and local authority about the report. The head is allowed to be accompanied by a union representative or colleague at any meeting s/he is asked to attend with a representative panel of the governing body to discuss the local authority report.

The chair must notify the local authority in writing of the action s/he intends to take, but the chair is not obliged to take any particular action indicated by the local authority. In particular, s/he is under no obligation to commence disciplinary or dismissal proceedings, although there may be insurance implications to consider. The chair should always take a local authority report seriously, examine carefully the evidence for raising the concern, and give the local authority a properly considered response. But the final decision as to what action to take lies with the governing body. In most policies, it is the chair who initiates any formal proceedings concerning the head including, in extreme situations, suspension.

Concerns raised by a regional schools commissioner

In academies, the DfE rather than the local authority would raise the issues with the board of trustees on behalf of the secretary of state. This would most probably be via the regional schools commissioner (RSC); however, the Education Skills Funding Agency (ESFA) may raise concerns, especially if the issues are financial. In MATs, the overarching academy trust will have a role in identifying performance issues relating to the headteacher.

Checklist: the chair, the headteacher and accountability

- Have you ever had the conversation with your headteacher as to what s/he expects from you and what you expect from her/him?
- Does the arrangement for keeping in touch suit both parties?
- Does the headteacher accept the role of the governing board in challenging her/him?
- Have you ever been on joint training, for example, about accountability, with your headteacher?
- Do the senior leaders have the external support they need to do their job well? In particular human resources advice, legal advice, procurement support? These are not jobs the governors should be doing, but the professional staff need to have external support to hand.
- Are you encouraging your middle and senior leaders to become governors at other schools to develop their understanding of governance in practice?
- Is the governing board equipped to deal with the headteacher's appraisal?
- Has the governing board considered succession planning for the headteacher's post?
- If you are governing in a federation or MAT, are the lines of accountability for each school's performance clear?
- Have you discussed the headteacher's development needs or aspirations with him/her?
- Have you asked the headteacher about her/his well-being?
- Have you and the headteacher looked at the Headteacher Standards together?

Leading school improvement

Improving the school(s) is the core business of the governing board and the aim of the school's or trust's strategy. In this chapter we cover the basic tools a chair must ensure the governing board has at its disposal, and briefly introduce the issues that the chair should put to the governing board to consider. Good governance, by definition, should lead to improvement rather than decline and failure.

Underperforming schools tended to have weak governance. Ofsted's annual report 2016/17 explained a little more about what was happening when governance fails. When reviewing inspections of 'requires improvement' schools, it stated: "Weak governance was a common feature. The main weaknesses included:

- not challenging effectively or holding leaders to account (for instance, by being too accepting of what they were told)
- not understanding school performance or quality well enough
- not holding leaders to account for the use of additional funding (such as the pupil premium)
- failing to act swiftly enough to challenge or support
- not checking the quality and impact of external support
- some governors lacked the confidence, skills and understanding to carry out their role effectively

This is not to say that weak governance is only found in schools where pupils are not progressing as they should. Some schools in challenging circumstances have governing boards that are instrumental in making sure change happens. In many cases, governance structures and personnel have been revised in response to declining standards, leading to transformed performance. In order to ensure we do not continue to have schools routinely underperforming, we need to improve the ways in which governing boards drive and monitor school improvement.

High expectations

Boards must be ambitious for all children and young people and infused with a passion for education and a commitment to continuous school improvement that enables the best possible outcomes. Governance must be grounded in reality as defined by both high-quality objective data and a full understanding of the views and needs of pupils, staff, parents, carers and local communities

DfE competencies for a chair: part 4

- promotes the importance of data interrogation to hold executive leaders to account
- is proactive in sharing good practice and lessons learned where these can benefit others and the organisation
- demonstrates how stakeholder concerns and questions have shaped board discussions, if not necessarily the final decision
- when appropriate, seeks external professional advice, knowing where this advice is available from and how to go about requesting it
- understands leadership and management processes and tools that support organisational change

- adopts and strategically leads a systematic approach to change management that is clear, manageable and timely
- ensures the board is aware of, and prepared for, formal external scrutiny
- is confident in providing strategic leadership to the board during periods of scrutiny
- is open to providing peer support to other chairs and takes opportunities to share good practice and learning
- is proactive in seeking and maximising opportunities for partnership working where these are conducive to achieving the agreed strategic goals

DfE Governance Handbook

In its 2012 Framework, Ofsted increased its inspection emphasis on governance. Its annual report 2012/13 said: "An effective chair promotes a culture of continuous evaluation and aspiration for improvement. S/he will eliminate defensiveness and complacency. S/he also ensures the governing board has the information it requires to fulfil its function… In the best schools, strong leaders and governors routinely challenge low expectations and mediocre teaching… Good governance is crucial to tackling underperformance and supporting improvement. Governance that is weak does not challenge the school about its performance or press the school to increase its aspirations."

The role of the governing board in setting the culture of the organisation (as covered in chapter 1.8) is important in first achieving a common understanding of the expectations and then leading to improved outcomes for pupils. Complacency at schools with intakes beginning from a higher point in more affluent areas, and demoralisation at schools in deprived areas with struggling intakes already at a disadvantage, can both lead to a lowering of expectations. This is compounded by the fact that Ofsted inspections do not appear to always recognise the additional work and ingenuity required in challenging communities.

5.1 Knowing the school(s)

The paradox is that boards need to get a close-up understanding of the operation in order to be able to stand back and play a productive role at a higher level. Without some organisational and sector knowledge, the board's decisions will lack context and could be misguided. But the closer the board gets to the everyday operations, the more anxious the senior staff become about unwelcome interference, and the greater the risk that some board members will start seeing only the trees and not the woods. Getting involved in the detail is seductive – it is a lot easier than dealing with the bigger issues.

David Fishel, Boards That Work: a guide for charity trustees

It is vital that the members of the governing board understand the school(s) and their strengths and weaknesses in order to make strategic decisions about current priorities and the future. The chair needs to ensure that the governing board has access to a range of information to help its understanding of the school, as well as the skills to understand and interrogate the information. Governing boards are expected, including by Ofsted, to 'triangulate' the information given, ie compare three different sources to see if they are all telling the same story. For example, if it is reported that teaching is consistently good, but pupil progress is not, questions must be asked.

If you are governing more than one school in a federation or a multi academy trust (MAT) then you should be given equivalent, consistent data across all the schools; this will be extremely useful in comparing the schools.

Data

In terms of educational performance, key information includes:

- The Department for Education's (DfE) Analyse School Performance (ASP) service, which can be used alongside the school performance tables publicly available on the web. Governors/trustees will require secure access approved via the school to view anonymised ASP data, which will also be available to Ofsted, local authorities, MATs and dioceses. Governors/trustees can view and analyse details on key headline measures, and compare performance at school and pupil group level against national averages and over time.

- There are a number of commercial products available to provide more detailed analyses and dashboard, including FFT Aspire Governor Dashboard, which was developed with NGA to highlight key measures.

- Regular attainment, progress, attendance and behaviour data for current pupils in all year groups, plus equivalent data for specific groups of pupils such as those deemed to be disadvantaged (if the group size is significant enough to be meaningful).

- Results of performance management of staff (how many staff met their objectives/how challenging their objectives were) and what CPD has been undertaken to what effect.

Different levels of data can be required for different purposes. More in-depth data will be required by any committee considering pupil progress and attainment in detail. Pupil progress data will be regularly collected by staff and its appropriateness for all purposes, including the governing board, should be reviewed to make sure staff are not being asked to collect data that is not useful. The chair needs to understand the data and be able to assess whether the governing board is receiving the right data. This assessment should be done in conjunction with the governor/trustee who leads on pupil data, who may be the chair of a standards committee.

The information presented should allow governors to understand the impact of different strategies employed to improve pupils' learning and to develop staff. However, it is important that the governing board is not only considering data concerning attainment in tests and qualifications.

As important as these are, there are other skills and qualities that the school aims for pupils to acquire. Measuring these will be more difficult, but it is important for the governing board to consider. It is also important that hard data is supplemented by information from visiting the school and the views of pupils, parents and staff. We return to the issue of triangulation in chapter 6. The DfE has produced a guide on its website for governors and trustees on understanding data, which everyone joining a governing board should be asked to read.

Headteacher's reports

The chair's relationship with the headteacher/chief executive, who is responsible for providing access to much of this information, is vital (see chapter 4.1). The senior leader's report to the governing board should summarise key information in a useful fashion, and in a format that relates to the priorities in the school's strategy. The governing board should have set out clear expectations for what the headteacher's report should cover. A new chair, at the beginning of her/his tenure, may want to review this with the headteacher.

For example, it is important that benchmarking information – comparable information from other schools – is provided. Much is now available in the performance tables on the DfE website, both on attainment and on finances. It is also important that all levels of the school – including the governing board – make use of research evidence and good practice from other places, in particular those practices with strong evidence of impact. There are a number of sources of this information that school leaders could be expected to quote, such as the Education Endowment Foundation.

Visiting the school

The chair should consider which school functions to attend – concerts and plays, awards and prize-giving, sports days, parents' evenings, open days, etc – and should encourage other governors to do so too. This may be partly to learn about and understand the school more fully, but also to represent the governing board, ensuring it is visible and listening to what staff, parents and pupils say about their school. Attending only celebration events can provide a partially obscured view of how the school operates. It is vitally important the chair (and other governors) have a much broader understanding of the school and the views of its stakeholders.

The chair with a good knowledge of the school can decide whether s/he needs to continue to undertake formal visits as other governors do (see NGA's guidance on visiting your school), and if so, the specific purpose of each visit. During COVID-19, understanding the layout of the premises also proved to be useful for testing risk assessments. When governors visit the school they will have some contact with staff, but it may often be senior leaders. The chair needs to discuss with the headteacher how the governing board might gain a better understanding of the staff team, its views and its morale. Understanding the climate of an organisation is critical for the board (see opposite).

Regular visits are unlikely to be practical for trustees of large MATs, so it is important that the chair leads a discussion at the board meeting as to how trustees will gain an understanding of the schools within their trust. This should involve dialogue with the academy committees, and it is good practice for the chair of the trust board to meet with the chairs of academy committees.

Parents, carers and pupils

The voices of parents, carers and pupils should be sought and valued by schools. It is important that the views of parent governors are not taken as representing the parent body as a whole; it is not their role to provide a 'parent view'. The chair needs to ensure that the governing board is aware of the range of views of parents and carers; discussion needs to be had about how to ensure the views of parents are collected and reported to the board. If this includes open meetings with parents, it is likely that the chair will play a part in leading those, but if there are a range of smaller focus group or consultative meetings with parents, they can be led by others. There is more information at www.nga.org.uk/Knowledge-Centre, including guidance jointly produced with ParentKind.

Chairs of boards also need to ensure that the views of pupils are sought. This does not happen as often as it should do, but with the Ofsted framework from September 2019 putting more reliance on feedback from pupils, this is no longer such an alien concept for school staff.

Ensuring boards listen to parents and pupils can be especially important when governing more than one school without school-level committees – in these situations it is easy for groups to feel isolated and ignored. MAT boards understandably tend to rely on information on parental and pupil views from academy committees, but the chair of the MAT board needs to ensure that this dialogue takes place, is effective and reported to trustees in a way that helps their decision-making.

Understanding the community

❝ All boards should assure themselves that mechanisms are in place for their organisation to engage meaningfully with all parents and carers. Parents and carers should be able to use these mechanisms to put forward their views at key points in their child's education. Boards should aim to build productive relationships, not only with parents and carers but also with the local community to create a sense of trust and shared ownership of the organisation's strategy, vision and operational performance. ❞

DFE Governance handbook

Children, and as a consequence the schools they attend, have very different starting points, and their families may have additional needs. This context is important for the chair – and the governing board – to be aware of, not to lower expectations but to understand the full role of schools at the heart of their community and the range of work that staff are increasingly called on to do. Although the mission of the school or trust is education; the way in which the schools have to achieve the same level of education will differ in different communities, especially as other public and third sector services supporting children and their families are shrinking.

5.2 Staff

Staff often like governors to be visible in school, but this may not always be possible due to time constraints. The chair however should consider accompanying the headteacher when very significant information is being given to the staff group, such as a staff restructuring process.

Governors may know members of staff who have presented to the governing board or as part of a monitoring exercise, but the chair needs to ensure there are systematic ways of obtaining staff views. Staff governors do not perform that function; they are not representing the staff body as a whole. It is important that information is obtained from members of staff, other than those on the senior leadership team, but this is a sensitive area and must not be done in a way that undermines the headteacher and the senior leadership team. Staff surveys are now common, but the information then needs to influence decision-making where relevant and the results reported back to the staff.

No school can be successful without good staff. Governing boards must be aware of their duties in relation to staffing to ensure the school stays on track and delivers the best outcomes for its pupils. With staffing accounting for around 75-85% of annual school revenue expenditure, as well as being the main resource for achieving the vision of the school, staffing is the largest and most significant ongoing investment any school will make. Governing boards are the employers of staff in academy trusts and voluntary aided schools, and act as though they are the employers in other maintained schools. The chair needs to be aware of those legal and moral responsibilities, which are critical to all aspects of achievement.

Staff morale and the climate in the school

The board must have a way of ascertaining staff morale and whether staff are on board with the school's vision and strategy. Data such as staff turnover and receiving exit interview reports will contribute, but a survey may also be useful. The chair presenting on the role of the governing board at a staff meeting could be helpful and a governor being present to listen when staff contribute to, for example, the school's strategy.

Recruitment of other staff

Governors need to be involved with the appointment of deputy heads and in most schools it will be appropriate for at least one governor or trustee to be involved in other senior leadership recruitment, including the school business manager. Appointment below senior leadership level is outside the governing board's strategic remit. Some governors argue that their involvement in other recruitment processes is necessary as they provide the HR expertise, and some heads who do not feel confident with HR agree with this view. This should be a matter of concern and identifies two problems.

The first is an area of development for the headteacher, and probably other senior leaders, so that they can carry out their management function. The second is whether the school has adequate HR support and expertise, both knowledge within the staff group and specialised external expertise to call upon when required. A headteacher must not rely on this being available within the governing board. Where there is additional expertise on the governing board this is helpful for its monitoring and evaluating function, but it does not negate the fact that the school must have its own HR function in which the governing board has confidence.

Involvement of governors in the recruitment of support staff is particularly common in small primary schools where the leadership capacity can be limited, but this should be resisted where possible as it is outside the board's strategic remit. It is not an expected component of the governing board's role, and the chair needs to ensure that both the head and governors understand this. A request from a headteacher to sit on an interview panel should be challenged as to why it is not possible for senior and middle leaders to manage this recruitment. It is likely that management responsibilities, especially at middle leadership level, may need to be reviewed by the governing board as a whole and continuing professional development (CPD) provided. Alternatively, there may be advantages to joining a group of schools, a federation or a MAT, with central HR support.

Performance appraisal

A maintained school governing body must have a policy in place setting out how teacher performance appraisal is carried out at the school. Appraisal should cover the development needs and objectives of a member of staff, and the chair might want to check that this is done and done well, as the appraisal process in many schools is not the positive process it can be for staff.

While there are currently no regulations covering performance appraisal of support staff, it is good practice and the school should have a policy and procedures in place. If this is lacking it may suggest a general lack of HR competence within the school, and the chair should ask questions as to HR management experience. This is frequently a weak point in school management and is often overlooked by governing boards. It is fairly common for chairs to be drawn into HR issues sooner than policies would require; HR should be largely the domain of senior leaders. Even when the board is legally the employer, managing staff is not a governance role, but the chair needs to have confidence that the headteacher has the necessary competence and would expect to be informed if disciplinary or capability proceedings were begun on any member of staff.

Pay progression for all teachers is directly linked to performance, and governing bodies need to monitor the outcomes of performance appraisals and their relationship to pay levels. Even though the regulations do not apply to academies, Ofsted still expects those governing to understand the link between teachers' pay and performance.

Pay progression for all teachers is directly linked to performance, and governing bodies need to monitor the outcomes of performance appraisals and their relationship to pay levels. Even though the regulations do not apply to academies, Ofsted still expects those governing to understand the link between teachers' pay and performance.

Staff development

Professional development of staff, often termed CPD, is a fundamental part of school improvement, and is likely to feature in a school's strategic priorities. However, governing boards do not tend to consider CPD as much as its importance would perhaps warrant. A lot of work is currently being carried out about the impact of CPD, for example, by the Teacher Development Trust. This shows that a number of factors are important: the long-term nature of CPD, which is relevant rather than one-size-fits-all, has a coherent programme structure, includes subject knowledge, subject-specific pedagogy, explicit discussions, experimenting, testing ideas using evidence and data, the right kind of external input, collaboration and peer learning. The support of school leaders is crucial.

5.3 Challenge and questioning

Governing boards are expected to question the information given to them by school and trust leaders. This is one of the prime functions of governors and trustees, and the chair must ensure that members of the governing board are equipped to ask good questions. Research has shown that governing boards have not always been as good at this as they should be, but the State of School Governing 2014 survey showed there had been improvements over the previous six years. The governing board needs to question itself as well as senior leaders. The chair must ensure that those who challenge do so appropriately and are not isolated or regarded as disruptive (see chapter 3.2 and 3.3 on creating a healthy culture).

A question can land differently depending on who is asking it and who it is directed at. The way in which we ask a question can have a large impact on the way in which it is perceived and therefore answered, or not. Competitive or co-operative questions may elicit different reactions. A competitive question about a headteacher's proposal might be styled "Is this going to work?". On the other hand, a question framed co-operatively as "How do we make this work?" would not imply scepticism about the plan, and therefore might result in a less defensive discussion about the pros and cons. Of course, there will be times when a governor does not think that the plan is up to scratch, and the chair must allow questions that will probe the issues well and expect answers to be given.

Ofsted carried out an exploration of what goes wrong in declining schools, which showed that problems start when processes to ensure accountability or drive change falter. Governors unaware of the issues facing the school and failing to provide sufficient challenge tended to be found in two situations: they were either over-reliant on the headteacher for knowledge of the school or displayed a lack of urgency due to complacency or distractions.

Over-reliance on the headteacher for knowledge of the school developed as a result of:

- misplaced loyalty
- excessive trust or too friendly
- headteacher providing unbalanced information

- lack of external evidence
- lack of own monitoring and information
- governors lacking data skills and training
- low aspirations from a lack of understanding by governors of how good other schools are

This underlines the importance of multiple sources of information.

Lack of urgency due to complacency or distractions correlated with:

- chair of the board in post a long time and 'world has moved on'
- governing board not strategic or evaluative in thinking
- governing board diverted by building plans, falling rolls, academisation, etc
- internal 'turbulence' in leadership and/or the governing boards.

Both were found to result in a governing board failing to challenge a well-established incumbent headteacher until it is too late or being unable to handle the transition to new leadership.

Key questions for governing boards to ask their headteachers

Chairs of governors will not go far wrong if these key questions are kept at the forefront of their planning and conversations with the vice chair, committee chairs and clerk. NGA members can also access the sub-set of follow-on questions in the guidance centre:

1. What are the school's values and do we have a clear vision and strategy? Are they reflected in our long-term development plans?
2. What are we doing to raise standards for all children, and are we making best use of the pupil premium?
3. Have we got the right approach to staffing?
4. Do we have a sound financial strategy, make the most efficient use of our resources, obtain good value for money and have robust procurement and financial systems?
5. Are the buildings and other assets in good condition and are they well used?
6. How well does the curriculum provide for and stretch all pupils?
7. How well do we keep parents informed and take account of their views?
8. Do we keep pupils safe and healthy?
9. How does the school promote good behaviour to enhance learning?
10. Do we offer a wide range of extra-curricular activities that engage all pupils?

5.4 School improvement support

Maintained schools may still look for advice from the local authority, although their capacity might be limited. MATs should provide school improvement support to their schools, as they are part of one organisation. Sharing capacity, good practice and benchmarking information across the MAT or federation can be an important driver of improvement. Schools that do not have this advantage of being part of a formal group of schools should also look to obtain this sort of information and support from other collaborations and alliances.

Your school should be and is very likely to be involved in a large number of collaborations, clusters and partnerships. Much of this will be the preserve of the headteacher and members of the teaching staff, but the governing board should be aware of their existence, aim, impact and the amount of time being devoted to them. Chairs of all types of school should also ensure that the leadership team is contributing to and engaging with all the support available to them, both through local partners and national initiatives.

If your school is 'outstanding', it is likely that it has been asked to support another school, and governors should approach this discussion with an awareness of the national approach to school-to-school improvement. Schools that provide this support often gain as much from the process as the school receiving the support. Ventures with significant implications – such as school leaders taking on additional responsibilities – require a decision of the governing board. Furthermore, the governing board may see a contribution to the wider system and pupils outside their school(s) as a good thing to do if resources permit. It may also provide development opportunities for middle as well as senior leaders.

All school leaders and governing boards should seek external advice and validation of the trust's or school's improvement strategies. The chair should take a lead role in ensuring that the governing board has access to appropriate external school improvement advice and that any external adviser makes at least an annual report to a governing board meeting. It is important that the chair, or another delegated governor, is included in other key discussions with the external adviser. This is separate to the external advice the governing board has as part of the headteacher's appraisal (see chapter 4.4), but the same person may be contracted by the governing board to perform both tasks.

Governing boards should know whether the school is involved in peer review and evaluation of any aspect of professional work by others working in the same field. There are many organisations that provide school improvement support and advice, often with their own frameworks, criteria and methodology, often including peer review.

Peer review is sometimes set up to be a reciprocal arrangement but not usually those who know the school well, and other times involving more of an expert facilitator.

The chair should consider collaboration at governing board level (see chapter 2.3). NGA can facilitate a peer review of governance. National leaders of governance (NLGs) are also available to support and mentor chairs free of charge (see chapter 8). At the time of writing, the NLG programme is under review for the school year beginning in September 2021.

Sustainable improvement

Much has been written about how to achieve sustainable improvement in schools and across groups of schools, which is beyond the scope of this handbook. However, the chair will want to check that the headteacher/CEO is aware of the literature and any accompanying research as there are many players in the system who attempt to persuade that their solution is the one to invest in. The matrix below, developed by Professor Toby Greany of the University of Nottingham during research on groups of schools, provides a useful overview to the non-educationalist, which will be familiar from other fields.

Teaching schools

These are outstanding schools that have been nationally recognised for their capacity to support and help other schools to improve educational outcomes through:

- the delivery of high-quality, evidence-based CPD
- the recruitment and training of new teachers
- sharing their best leaders to coach and mentor staff in other schools

- acting as a catalyst for school-to-school partnerships that provide school improvement support, often to those who need it most

There should be at least one teaching school within reasonable distance of the school. The teaching school alliance is the group of schools and other partners that works with or is supported by the teaching school. Some teaching school alliances work in a more collaborative way than others and some teaching schools are more successful than others. The governing board should ask which alliances the school is part of and to what effect, and whether the level of engagement is correct.

The DfE is now funding six new teaching school hubs as part of a 'test and learn' programme to reform teaching schools and the wider approach to system leadership. The new hubs will be expected to work with between 200 and 300 schools, providing support to regional schools in three main areas: school-to-school support, continuing professional development, and teacher recruitment and retention.

DfE school improvement offer

This is a government programme created to assist struggling schools that receive at least one 'requires improvement' (RI) judgment, with funding increasing with further RI judgments from Ofsted. The Teaching School Council aims to ensure that eligible schools are provided with the best possible support from National Leaders of Education (NLEs).

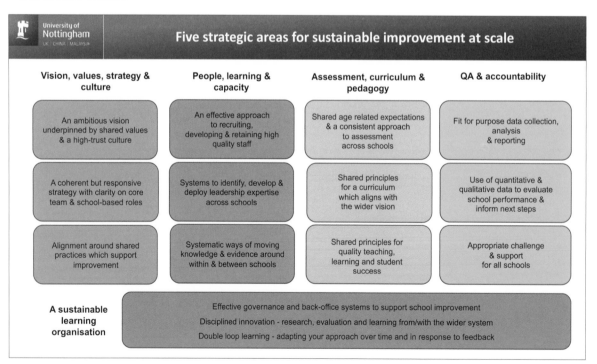

Greany, T. (2018) Sustainable improvement in multi-school groups

The local authority, the diocese and the regional schools commissioner

Much of the contact from the local authority and, where relevant, the diocesan authority, is of an operational or professional nature and is rightly the concern of the headteacher. Issues can then be raised in the regular meetings between the head and the chair. However, some specific matters will be strategic and the concern of the governing board. The local authority might signal governor-level matters, but the chair should always be alert, as governors can often be overlooked. For example, at present the issue of whether or not a maintained school should convert to academy status or join a group of schools in a federation or a MAT is a decision for the governing board, but some local authorities and some DfE staff have chosen to speak only to heads. Similarly, approaches from the regional schools commissioner might be made initially to the trust staff, but it will almost always be appropriate to include the chair and possibly others on the board in such discussions.

Other relevant issues include any plans that may affect the future of the school, such as possible reorganisations, significant changes in pupil rolls, and major changes to the financial regime. The chair may then need to represent the governing board at meetings with these authorities. Some of these issues will apply to academies too, and the local authority should have mechanisms for communicating with academies as well as maintained schools.

5.5 Ofsted inspections

Governors should be aware that inspectors assess four key elements of a school:

- the quality of education
- personal development
- behaviour and attitudes
- leadership and management (which includes governance)

Inspectors consider whether leaders, including those responsible for governance:

- have high expectations of and high ambitions for all pupils in the school, including those who are harder to reach
- create coherence and consistency across the school so that pupils benefit from effective teaching and consistent expectations, wherever they are in the school
- seek to engage parents and their community thoughtfully and positively in a way that supports pupils' education
- focus their attention on the education provided by the school

- take into account the workload and well-being of their staff
- develop and strengthen the quality of the workforce, including high-quality continuing professional development

During the lead inspector's initial call to the headteacher s/he will establish what the governance structure of the school is, with reference to the range of functions delegated to academy committees within MATs. The chair has a key role during an Ofsted inspection. S/he will need to ensure that the governing board is aware that the inspection is taking place, and that the head has made arrangements for the Ofsted team to meet representative governors. If at all possible, the chair should make her/himself available to meet the inspector(s) and may need to suggest times s/he is available. Ideally, the vice chair and chair of any key committees should also attend the meeting. Inspectors will do all they can to accommodate the availability of governors. The chair could ask to attend Ofsted's final team meeting with the headteacher; this is not standard practice but it does provide a much better understanding of the inspection findings. Governors must be encouraged to attend the final feedback session, which can be minuted by the clerk.

The chair, with the help of the clerk and the headteacher, needs to be familiar with the content of the Ofsted handbook and in particular its expectations of governors. NGA's knowledge centre provides a summary of the handbook and other guidance for governors preparing for inspection.

In practice, Ofsted inspectors vary slightly in their approach to governors; some raise the full list of issues covered in the Ofsted guidance, whereas others might concentrate on a few issues, such as the strengths and weaknesses of the school; safeguarding; and the governing board's role in developing the curriculum. Governors should be prepared to answer questions about how they carry out their role in terms of ensuring compliance, how they monitor the work of the school, how they challenge the school and what training they have had. It should not be a memory test, but governors should be able to demonstrate awareness of the key issues in the school strategy and the reasons for prioritising them.

The Ofsted judgment

A large majority (86%) of schools are judged to be 'good' or 'outstanding', If the school is judged 'outstanding', there are a number of opportunities for the school, including that as a chair you could consider applying to become a national leader of governance (see chapter 8). You could also consider your job well done, and think about whether your governance experience might now be better used at a school that is 'inadequate' or 'requires improvement'. Where a school is judged to 'require improvement', it is eligible for the DfE's support offer (see above).

When Ofsted judges a school 'inadequate', it places the school in a category of concern, either serious weaknesses or requiring special measures. The secretary of state will issue an academy order to an 'inadequate' maintained school, which will then become a sponsored academy. Ofsted will monitor an 'inadequate' academy unless it is re-brokered to a new MAT.

5.6 Leading change

Many schools are considering changes to their structure, usually whether or not to join a MAT or possibly a move to a federation (for maintained schools). Unless a school is not performing well, it is the governing body that decides if it should become an academy. To help schools exploring that option, NGA has published a series called Taking the Next Steps alongside the Association of School and College Leaders and Browne Jacobson. Other partnerships are being started to provide services to schools, many of which require representation from member schools.

Some schools are requested to take an increased number of pupils, while others may have to cope with a falling roll. There will be other changes that could impact on the school's future, for example, changes to the funding formula used to distribute government funding to schools. The chair needs to ensure that the governing board is briefed on relevant changes, and understands the world of education outside its gates.

The board's annual strategy discussion with the senior leaders (see chapter 5.1) should be an important driver of change, or at least ensure debate. The use of a PESTLE (Political, Economic, Social, Technological, Legal, Environmental) or a SWOT (Strengths, Weaknesses, Opportunities, Threats) analysis will initiate a focus on external factors for those governing boards that have a tendency to only look inwards.

As in many organisations, governing boards often struggle to explore or lead change within their school, preferring to manage the status quo. However, with funding still tight over the next few years for many schools, seeking efficiencies might continue to drive change. As well as ensuring the governing board has the relevant information at its disposal, the chair has to encourage a culture of open minds, creativity and exploration. This can be difficult when governing boards also have important fiduciary duties and may therefore tend to be cautious in order to ensure these are met. A healthy board includes people who understand

and approach risk in different ways, and someone with expertise in change management can help the chair in setting a dynamic culture.

 Checklist: leading school improvement

- Is the governing board's business focused on the key priorities in the school strategy?
- Is the school's self-evaluation process robust, and is the governing board appropriately engaged at a strategic level in the whole process?
- Is the headteacher's report to the governing board structured around the strategic priorities, and do these form the main headings of the school's development plan?
- Does the governing board receive the ASP reports and a relevant dashboard with benchmarking data?
- Does the governing board have the skills to understand and question the data being presented, or does it need independent advice on what the data means?
- Does the governing board have progress data for current pupils reported to it as well as attainment?
- Does the governing board know which groups of children in the school are not doing as well as they should? Who are they, and why aren't they doing as well?
- How does the governing board seek views from parents?
- How does the governing board seek views from students?
- How does the governing board seek views from staff?
- Do you have a visits protocol, and does it make clear that the purpose of the visit needs to be linked to the priorities being monitored by the governing board?
- Did the governors speak to the Ofsted inspectors and receive a report from them?
- Has the governing board considered the collaborations that the school is involved with and what impact they have had?
- What evidence has been used to develop the school improvement approach?
- Has the capacity for sustainable school improvement been demonstrated?
- What school improvement support is being accessed and has the governing board received a report from any external agency?
- Has the governing board considered whether joining a group of schools might improve the pupils' education?
- Is the governing board receptive to discussions about change and willing to explore options for doing things differently in order to improve the school?

Leading governing board business

6

The focus of the business of the governing board must be school improvement without neglecting the compliance activities for which it has responsibility, such as financial oversight and probity.

Just because the governing board has a legal responsibility for ensuring something is done, this does not mean governors or trustees should do the task themselves. Governing boards should seek to delegate to senior leaders as much as possible of what is neither strategic nor scrutiny of the executive.

An effective chair has to:

- in cooperation with the clerk, establish effective working procedures and sound committee structures
- ensure that the governing board meets all its legal responsibilities, while continuing to focus on its three core functions (see chapter 1.1)

- chair governing board meetings effectively, ensuring that all members have the opportunity to contribute while completing the business in a timely fashion
- make decisions only in cases of emergency and keep the governing board fully informed

The chair must ensure that the business of the governing board is focused around the school's priorities, as set out in the most recent school strategy. For an introduction to a school strategy, see chapter 1.6 and download a free copy of Being Strategic: a guide for governing boards from www.nga.org.uk. Key stakeholders need to be involved.

DfE competencies for a chair: part 5

- leads board meetings in a way that embodies the culture, values and ethos of the organisation
- values the importance of the clerk/governance professional and their assistance in the coordination of leadership and governance requirements of the organisation
- sets sufficiently high expectations of the clerk/governance professional, as applicable, ensuring the board is compliant with the regulatory framework for governance
- works with the clerk to ensure the right data is provided by executive leaders, which is accessible to the board and open to scrutiny
- listens to the clerk/governance professional and takes direction from them on issues of compliance and other matters
- ensures the board understands the scope of issues in question and is clear about decisions they need to make
- leads the board to identify when specialist skills and experience in audit, fraud or human resources are required either to undertake a specific task or more regularly lead committees of the board

- summarises the position in order to support the board to reach consensus where there are diverging views
- ensures that different perspectives, viewpoints and dissenting voices are properly taken into account and recorded
- facilitates decision-making even if difficult and manages the expectations of executive leaders when doing so
- recognises the limits of any discretionary chair's powers and uses them under due guidance and consideration and with a view to limiting such use
- ensures the board seeks guidance from executive leaders or others in the senior leadership team and from the clerk/governance professional before the board commits to significant or controversial courses of action
- leads the board and challenges leaders appropriately in setting risk appetite and tolerance, and knows when the board needs external expert advice on risk management
- ensures that the board has sight of, and understands, organisational risks and undertakes scrutiny of risk management plans

Key steps in the annual strategic cycle

Step one: where are we now?
Carry out an evaluation – how well does the school perform now? SWOT (Strengths, Weaknesses, Opportunities, Threats) and PESTLE (Political, Economic, Social, Technological, Legal, Environmental) analyses can be useful. Review against last year's strategy if you had one.

Step two: what's the vision?
The vision should, in a few sentences, describe what pupils will leave the school knowing, being and having done.

The vision's aim should be to continuously improve, and make the experience of the school the very best it can be for pupils, parents and staff. Projecting forward a few years, what specific goals do you want the school/trust and its pupils to have achieved? There is no need to rewrite the vision annually, but it is good practice to review it.

Step three: what are the obstacles in the way of achieving our vision?
You need to identify the challenges and potential obstacles to achieving the vision in order to plan around them. Concentrate on overcoming those that are most important and likely to have the most impact on the children's learning or your other identified goals. The risks both of making change and of no change need to be identified.

Step four: what are our strategic priorities?
The school's strategy should include a small number of key priorities – between four and six. These need to be ambitious but also achievable with focused attention and determination.

Step five: what are our resources?
Having identified the vision and the priorities, you need to identify the resources you already have and any you will need in the future. It is important to tailor resources to the vision and the priorities, not the other way around. This might include a review of the staffing structure.

Step six: how will we know whether we are achieving the vision?
The school's strategy document needs to include what success looks like for each priority and what evidence is needed to measure progress. This should result in measures of what you value. It should all fit on no more than three sides of A4 paper. There is more guidance in Being Strategic: a guide for governing boards and school leaders.

Step seven: operational plan.
Having developed the vision and the strategy with the key priorities, this is no longer a governance task. You can hand the strategy over to the headteacher who, with the staff, will develop an operational plan – often called a school improvement plan (SIP) or school development plan (SDP) – and oversee its implementation. It is likely to be many pages of actions, including specific details of how it is going to be put into practice, by whom and when. The governing board does not need to monitor this full plan; the headteacher need only report by exception to the governing board – this means those activities where progress towards achieving the priorities is significantly higher or lower than expected. S/he may well already have discussed any of those issues with the chair at an early stage.

Step eight: what will we monitor?
Governing boards will scrutinise the progress towards achieving the strategic priorities regularly, at least termly at full governing board meetings. The headteacher's reports should be based on the measures set out in the strategy. In the meantime, if other unexpected issues arise, you need to consider how they fit with the vision and strategic priorities; if they don't fit well, why are you considering them? Do they need to be acted upon now? Why didn't we think about this when agreeing on the strategy? The priorities should also inform the business of any committees.

Step nine: where are we now?
Back to the beginning. Even though the strategy is for a three- (or five-) year period, progress will be evaluated and presented before the next annual strategy session, so that the review can take this into account and look again at the coming years. The governing board should agree on the format of the school self-evaluation, but the majority of the work will be carried out by senior leaders. Governors will want to ask searching questions to ensure it is an honest, accurate assessment, based on robust evidence.

The chair must make sure that the governing board is equipped to engage with the annual planning and review cycle. This should include an annual strategy session with other senior leaders. This may be a full away day or half-day session. When you are governing a federation, it is clear that the strategy will cover all the schools within the federation, whereas within a multi academy trust (MAT), the responsibilities can differ from one MAT to another with different levels of governance responsibility. These need to be made clear before any strategy session is planned.

It is entirely up to the school how it sets out its self-evaluation; what is important is that it is carried out and that it is accurate. The governing board needs to be closely involved in school self-evaluation so that it can set aims and objectives that will improve the school's performance. Risk analysis needs to form part of that evaluation.

6.1 Governing board committees

A few governing boards conduct almost all their business through full governing board meetings, although regulations dictate that panels have to deal with issues relating to staff appointments, grievance and discipline. Those boards that choose not to have committees have to meet more frequently, at least monthly.

However, most governing boards rely on a system of committees. Committees have to be established at full governing board meetings with defined membership and terms of reference, including specific delegation of tasks. Those terms of reference will specify whether the chairs of committees are elected or appointed by the chair or the board.

A model of two committees can be very effective for standalone schools:

- education committee (or an alternative name such as progress and attainment, or standards and curriculum) monitors and analyses all information relating to pupil outcomes
- a resources committee (covering finance, premises and personnel) has oversight of other organisational functions, including financial monitoring and the annual budget process, and health and safety

The committee structure within MATs is more complex, with academy committees (often called local governing bodies) as well as traditional committees including trustees. Consult your scheme of delegation and for further information, see Welcome to a Multi Academy Trust.

The chair needs to ensure that governing board meetings do not rerun discussions that have been had in committee meetings or in other ways duplicate the committees' business, which has been delegated. No committee structure will be perfect in perpetuity and the chair should ensure there is a discussion as to whether the previous year's structure should continue in the same way.

The board chair needs to appoint or encourage suitable people to put themselves forward to chair committees (see chapter 3.2) and should not chair committees her/himself. The chair of the committee then takes the lead both in organising the agenda and monitoring that actions are followed up, and also in considering the big issues that the committee's work covers.

The chair of the governing board does need to ensure the committees' roles are carried out effectively without taking on tasks that are rightly performed by school staff and that there is no duplication at board level. S/he shouldn't feel that s/he must attend or be a member of both committees. S/he does need to have an understanding of the committee's business, but can achieve this by reading the committee papers and discussing progress with the chairs of committees and the headteacher, acting as a sounding board and only intervening where absolutely necessary. A confident governing board chair will not feel threatened by chairs of the committees having a more thorough knowledge of an aspect of the school's business, such as the budget, but will know enough to ensure that part of the governing board's work is being carried out well by the committee on the board's behalf.

Chairs' committee

Governing boards sometimes establish a chairs' committee to include all chairs of committees. This has sometimes been called an executive group but it is an inappropriate title, given that it is the senior leadership team (SLT) who are the executive. Others have begun to call it a strategy group, but it should not have a role in setting strategy, which is the role of the full governing board. Rather, it should ensure that progress is being made since the last meeting and act as a sounding board.

Although it can be a forum for interesting, wide-ranging and in-depth discussions about possible strategies, this kind of grouping risks undermining the role of the full board by creating two tiers of governors. It is the chair's role to ensure that the ways of working are appropriate, efficient and do not exclude others from engaging. In practice, many governing boards have a small group of active governors who do much of the work, but the chair of the governing board needs to ensure all members are engaged and address any who are not contributing.

There is also a danger that a chairs' committee could overstep into the operational, particularly around staffing issues. Such a group will tend to consist of the more experienced or committed governors, who have a greater knowledge of the workings of the school. It can be useful to discuss issues that concern more than one committee, such as making the connection between the curriculum offer and the staffing structure, or the impact of the pupil premium expenditure, before proposals go to the full governing board for decision. However, although presenting proposals that have already been discussed by a chairs' committee may speed up decision-making at a full governing board meeting, other governors may not be fully informed about the background to key decisions.

If such a committee does exist in the school when the chair takes over, s/he should take the opportunity to review its remit and effectiveness, and discuss with other governors whether they are content with this division of roles. If it is considered necessary to delegate some of the governing board's functions to such a group, perhaps the governing board is simply too big to have useful discussions and reconstitution to a smaller size should be considered. On the other hand, termly meetings between the headteacher, deputy head, chair and vice chair can achieve the same result of ensuring the governing board is making the connections it needs to across the organisation and planning the work of the governing board without having any decision-making role or needing formal terms of reference.

Whatever structure is agreed by the governing board, it is the chair's role to ensure all governors contribute and that full discussion and decision-making take place in board meetings.

6.2 Financial oversight

This element of governance is probably the most different between academy trusts and maintained schools. The requirements of the company and charity law have been added to by the DfE as set out in the Education Skills and Funding Agency's (ESFA) Academies Financial Handbook (AFH). A chair of an academy trust should be familiar with the AFH. MATs vary as to how much financial monitoring is delegated to the academy committees; so far it is a minority of MATs that have centralised key financial tasks, such as budget setting. Local authority maintained schools have to submit a Schools Financial Value Standard (SFVS) return.

All schools, whatever their financial reporting mechanisms, will be dealing with the aftermath of austerity. Additional funding provided over the three-year period 2020-23 aims to cover:

- A growth in pupil numbers
- A real-terms protection of per-pupil funding
- Some additional funding for pupils with high needs
- The cost of increases to teachers' pay, including raising starting salaries for all new teachers to £30,000

Although governing boards report to NGA that balancing budgets is their top challenge, this is not universal and the extent of the challenge very much varies from place to place.

Over the past few years there has been much more information published by the DfE on its website to support governing boards in their financial responsibilities, on their role in resource management and obtaining efficiencies. There is also information as to how schools can use integrated curriculum and financial planning (ICFP) to create the best curriculum for pupils with available funding.

Whether or not the governing board chooses to have a resources or financial committee, the chair needs to ensure both that the whole board understands their financial responsibilities and that there are a couple of individuals on the board who have financial expertise.

Summary of top 10 'musts' for chairs of trusts and other trustees

Taken from the ESFA's Academies Financial Handbook

1. Apply highest standards of conduct and ensure robust governance
2. Ensure the board of trustees meets at least three times a year, and conducts business only when quorate
3. Approve a written scheme of delegation of financial powers
4. Manage conflicts of interest, be even-handed with related parties
5. Ensure the board approves a balanced budget for the financial year and minute their approval
6. Share management accounts with the chair of trustees monthly
7. Ensure decisions about executive pay follow a robust, evidence-based process
8. Appoint an audit and risk committee
9. Submit audited accounts to ESFA by 31 December
10. Ensure an appropriate, reasonable and timely response to findings by auditors, taking opportunities to strengthen financial management and control

6.3 The chair and the clerk

Every governing board must appoint, at a full governing board meeting, a clerk (in some academies the clerk is known as the company secretary or a number of other job titles together termed governance professionals) and all governing board meetings must be clerked. A meeting can take place without the clerk, but in that situation the governing board must appoint a governor to act as clerk for that meeting in order to allow it to take place. The head must not clerk a meeting and it is not good practice for the chair do so in the absence of the usual clerk.

A good clerk is an enormous asset, and building a good working relationship with the clerk must be an early objective for any new chair. The clerk has a clearly specified and important role in ensuring that the governing board performs its functions properly. Governors must take note of the advice of the clerk. Research shows an association between the effectiveness of the clerk and the effectiveness of the governing board. NGA has a model job description for a clerk and an academy governance professional at www.nga.org.uk/Roles-and-responsibilities.

The clerk's role requires a wide range of high-level skills and knowledge. NGA's guidance centre has a section on legislation, policies and procedures designed with the clerk in mind. It is important that the clerk is paid for enough hours to carry out not only the clerking of the main governing board meetings, but also any committees and all the associated administrative work such as conducting a skills audit. A clerk should be paid at a rate commensurate with the skills and knowledge required for the role.

A good clerk

- works well with the chair of governors (and chairs of any committees) and the headteacher to ensure that governing board business is conducted effectively
- provides sound advice to the governing board on governance, constitutional and procedural matters
- provides effective administrative support to all aspects of the governing board's work
- manages information effectively in accordance with legal requirements
- ensures the governing board is properly constituted
- has experience of good practice in other contexts, for example, through work with other governing boards

There are three main ways of obtaining a clerk; each has advantages and disadvantages:
- some local authorities and MATs provide a clerking service as a charged optional service to schools
- some governing boards employ an independent clerk
- some governing boards appoint a member of the school administrative staff to clerk their meetings and in some MATs these posts are supervised by a governance manager

If the governing board decides to consider appointing a member of the administrative staff, governors should interview for the role against a job description and a person specification. The work of a clerk should not be seen as part of another role in the school. If the clerk is employed in another role, s/he should have a separate contract of employment for her/his role as the clerk.

The clerk should be the constitutional conscience of the governing board. Their first loyalty must be to the whole governing board, not to the local authority, the diocese, the headteacher, or even the chair.

NGA recommends that clerks should have the benefit of appropriate development and training; a contract; a job description and person specification (if you do not have one, there is an example of each at www.nga.org.uk/clerking); and a pay grade appropriate to the post. A new chair of governors may wish to review these, as there is considerable poor practice in this area.

n|g|a 360°
for Clerks

A 360° appraisal provides a unique opportunity to gain valuable insights into your clerking strengths and development needs. Based on the DfE's Competency Framework for Clerks, it provides a comprehensive snapshot of your skills.

The appraisal is simple to set up and includes confidential feedback from your peers on various aspects of your role, as well as a mentoring session with an NGA consultant to guide you through the analysis of the report and the identification of key areas for development. Template documents to help you analyse your appraisal report and create a personal development plan are included in the package.

www.nga.org.uk/360

Where the clerk is employed directly by the governing board, the chair line manages the clerk and this should include an annual performance review. This review should be based on the school's annual performance review arrangements for support staff, and include any appropriate recommendation and decision regarding pay advancement. Where the clerk is employed through the local authority's clerking service or the MAT, the governing board should still conduct an annual feedback session with the clerk to ensure harmonious working; this could be with the chair or another member of the board.

A new chair should set an early meeting with the clerk in order to discuss the way in which the two roles work together; tasks in the annual calendar; the next agenda; any possible changes to ways of working; any training needs of either the clerk or the chair; and of course to get to know each other and each other's approaches. The clerk will need to inform any relevant bodies of the change of chair so that information is sent to the right person (this should include NGA if members). The chair will need to decide how and where they want communications sent, both electronic and paper: at home, via the clerk, or via the school, and if post sent to school should be saved up for collection when next in school.

Reducing paperwork

The biggest request from governors is the need to reduce the amount of paper they have to read in order to perform the role. This is a task that the chair and the clerk should discuss and take into their own hands. Some local authority clerks are given standard agendas that do not reflect the needs of the particular school; however, it is up to the board, led by the chair, to determine how they organise their paperwork.

School policies

Many governing boards complain about the amount of time spent on reviewing and approving school policies. This is an area where the chair needs to step in and ensure that the governing board keeps its strategic focus. Many documents referred to as policies are, in fact, a combination of policies and procedures. The policy should just be a (short) statement of intent – the principles – but it is almost always followed by a set of procedures on how it will be carried out. The latter are the business of school staff, although governing boards do need to approve any procedure (eg complaints or staff discipline appeals) in which they will be directly involved. The Department for Education (DfE) has clarified which policies are statutory requirements and who can sign them off.

The chair should ensure that the governing board (even when its membership includes relevant specialist expertise) is not actually writing policies. This is not a strategic use of time and confuses pro-bono work with the role of the board in ensuring that appropriate polices exist and are complied with. Being given long school 'policies' to in effect proofread is not governance. It is the role of governing boards to ensure that the senior leaders have developed policies, taking expert advice as required, and that these are reviewed as appropriate. The governing board should then monitor the impact of the agreed policies. Academy committees will not need to consider policies that have been agreed centrally by the board of trustees.

6.4 Governing board meetings

The law, or in the case of academies the articles of association, requires three full meetings of the governing board every school year. That alone is very unlikely to cover adequately the necessary business, and most governing boards plan more meetings, either of the full governing board or of committees with delegated responsibilities, or sometimes both. Boards without committees tend to meet monthly (with the exception of August).

Governing boards should think in terms of a yearly meeting cycle. Within that cycle, it is up to the chair to ensure that every meeting has a manageable agenda and that the year's business is properly transacted. Dates should be set well in advance and if meetings end up inquorate, this is a clear indication that the chair needs to consider the commitment of members of the board as well as the practical considerations of the time of day at which meetings are held.

All governors should be aware of how long the meeting may last. Two hours is common for a full governing board meeting. Shorter than this, and the business of the governing board is unlikely to be covered properly (unless meetings are more frequent than once a term). Much longer, and the effectiveness of the meeting is likely to reduce.

A key responsibility of the chair is to ensure there is a positive climate within the board by:

- keeping papers brief and focused

- expecting each board member to make a unique contribution

- maintaining high standards with regard to meeting preparation, conduct and output

- being clear about operational procedures and meeting conclusions

- praising and recognising the contributions of both board members and the executive

- creating a sense of pride in being a member of a top-class governance team

Sir Adrian Cadbury, Corporate Governance and Chairmanship

Preparation for a meeting

The chair should consider and approve the agenda for each meeting. S/he should seek suggestions from the head and the clerk. In addition, there needs to be a process for other governors to suggest items. However, it is critical that the chair ensures the majority of time in meetings is spent considering school improvement and the education being provided to pupils, while not overlooking financial and legal responsibilities. The school strategy should be seen as a central tool for the governing board and the headteacher's report should be focused on its key priorities.

Every agenda should include a chair's report, so that the chair gives a short oral or written account of any urgent actions (see chapter 6.6) s/he has had to take on the governing board's behalf since the last meeting. Under normal circumstances, it is likely that no action will have been taken since the last meeting, but it is good practice to remind the chair and the board that it is not the chair's place to be making decisions.

There may also be essential agenda items relating to initiatives and decisions made outside the school by government agencies and/or the local authority. There will be some standing items, such as matters arising from the minutes and training updates. Some chairs prefer to get those done at the top of the agenda, while others prefer to ensure substantive items take priority.

The clerk then circulates the agreed agenda to governors. Unless the meeting is urgent, regulations require the clerk of a governing body in a maintained school to issue the agenda at least seven days before the meeting. Academies' articles are likely to stipulate a time, sometimes 14 days.

Any papers, whether proposals or reports, that need to be considered in relation to agenda items must be high-quality and distributed at the same time. The authors of those papers should be invited to attend the meeting for that item: this is useful for middle leaders to experience how the governing board operates.

The chair may have commented on a draft version of the headteacher's paper if it is a controversial proposal or if the head struggles to understand the appropriate detail required in a report. Once a head understands what constitutes a good board paper, this should not generally be necessary.

The chair needs to ensure that information is coming from a number of sources, so that they can be compared and contrasted, without all of it being mediated by the headteacher/chief executive. This does not need to be big data, but may be observational or conversational data, for example, obtained from focus groups. This practice of triangulating information is crucial to effective governance but is quite often neglected.

Papers should not be tabled at the meeting itself. It is important that governors can read papers in advance and the meeting is not spent entirely with the head or others reporting orally to the governors. Despite having the law on their side, some clerks struggle to get senior leaders to do this, and chairs may need to intervene and make it clear that they will not accept tabled papers.

The chair is most likely to conduct the meeting successfully if s/he has mastered the content of the papers, formed a provisional view of the issues and considered the possible courses of action open to the governing board. It is usually a good idea for the chair to discuss the more complex or contentious items in advance of the meeting, for example, with the head, clerk or chair of any relevant committee. Some of the literature on board practice suggests that a chair should know the likely position of all members before the meeting begins, but moving too much of the conversation outside the formal meeting can lead to the perception of deals being done and issues stitched up beforehand, or an inner circle rather than a full team of equals.

Information for boards: triangulation

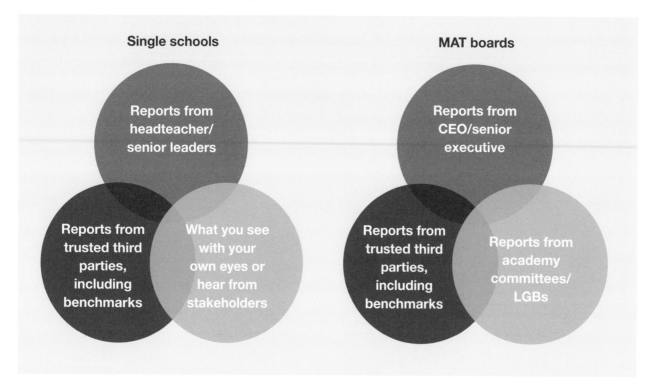

Single schools

Reports from headteacher/ senior leaders

Reports from trusted third parties, including benchmarks

What you see with your own eyes or hear from stakeholders

MAT boards

Reports from CEO/senior executive

Reports from trusted third parties, including benchmarks

Reports from academy committees/ LGBs

Minutes

All governing board meetings should be recorded by means of properly maintained minutes, which are public documents. It is the clerk's job to take the minutes, but it is the chair who is responsible for their accuracy. It is the chair's role to ensure that:

- minutes are checked as soon as possible after a meeting to ensure they present an accurate record of discussions and decisions
- appropriate action is taken if the minutes are not adequate
- minutes are circulated to governors within the timescale agreed by the governing board

Minutes should be a clear and concise record of the main points of a discussion at a meeting, the decisions made and any actions points decided on. Although they are not a word-by-word record of the meeting, minutes should specifically record when the governing board is asking challenging questions of the school, as this demonstrates that the governing board is carrying out its challenge function. Minutes do not have to be long, but should reflect the spirit of the discussion and be clear enough to be meaningful to someone who was not at the meeting.

At a well chaired meeting

- everyone has a voice but no one is allowed to dominate the discussion
- there is good time management, so the two hours or so are used constructively
- governors are clear whether items are for information or decision
- people leave the meeting confident and clear that they are doing the right job and doing it well, including the less articulate or less experienced governors

At a badly chaired meeting

- people do not have the information they need
- people are not given the opportunity to speak
- members' contributions are not relevant to the matters under discussion
- the chair allows the head to run the meeting
- important items are not given sufficient time in the meeting
- the agenda is not completed
- people leave the meeting unsure what has been agreed or achieved

6.5 Chairing the meeting

Chairing a formal meeting is a skill but one that can be acquired; there is no one style or method. Every chair will operate in slightly different ways with varying degrees of formality. Most new chairs of governing boards will have had experience as a chair of committee or a vice chair, if not from being chair of another school or even in another walk of life. However, if a new chair has no experience of chairing meetings, s/he may wish to attend a short training session or seek advice from an experienced chair.

> One is not to talk too much from the chair. As time goes by, it becomes more difficult to resist the temptation to reminisce, or bring the discussion at the board onto more familiar ground… the chairman's job is to listen, not to chatter. Chairs are there to orchestrate the discussion, so that it comes to a fruitful conclusion… Chairs need to integrate the skills and the perceptions of all those seated around the boardroom table. The chair's place in all this comes nearest to the conductor of an orchestra.

Sir Adrian Cadbury, Corporate Governance and Chairmanship

At the meeting, the chair has to secure the efficient coverage of business on the agenda, while maintaining or strengthening the governing board's sense of working as a team. The chair must ensure that no one, including the chair or head, dominates proceedings; that all who wish to express a view have the opportunity to do so without tedious repetition; and that, as far as possible, everyone feels comfortable with the decisions and understands their implications. The chair must ensure proportionate time is allowed for each item without leaving members feeling that some items have not been examined properly.

It must be assumed that board members have read papers in advance, and that if those papers fulfil their function, there should normally not be a reason for the author to present them orally at the meeting. This needs to be made clear in advance to prevent senior leaders spending time preparing presentations for which there is not time at the meeting, otherwise there is a danger that the senior leader perceives that the board is not considering sufficiently a paper they may have spent much time constructing. It is normal practice for the author to attend the discussion and respond to questions. Requests for further information may be entirely valid or may be a way to avoid making a difficult decision. The chair can seek the view of the rest of the board as to whether the decision needs to be deferred pending fuller information.

During a meeting the chair might need to seek the clerk's advice about a procedural issue. While a formal process can sometimes be useful to help resolve an issue within a meeting, often difficulties that arise during meetings are due to behaviour and the dynamics between the people involved in the discussion, and the chair will need to use emotional intelligence, influence and people skills.

Arriving at a decision

The board meeting is a forum for constructive compromise, but before that is reached, all differences must be aired and resolved. There is bound to be some ambiguity, some politics and a range of opinions. It is the job of the chair to ensure the discussion revolves around logical, objective analysis. Facts and evidence need to be well researched and presented.

A strong board is likely to contain strong personalities, and the chair needs to ensure that some members do not have undue influence. Those used to getting their own way cannot be allowed to achieve this without due consideration of the issue; some use charm and others appear more intimidating, but often powerful people do not relish challenge. The way to combat unwarranted entreaties and pressures is integrity, courage and good judgment.

Sometimes navigating to a resolution when there have been some unexpected interventions at a meeting will be required. A chair needs to be able to recognise the positions of all the parties and seek common ground. Summarising the discussion and drawing the appropriate conclusion is a very important responsibility of the chair.

The chair needs to be aware of the flow of the discussion and who has not spoken on each item. Tactics such as the chair going around the table asking each governor in turn to express a view can be useful when important decisions are being discussed. On some occasions, it may be necessary for the chair to play 'devil's advocate' to ensure that all governors have thoroughly understood the decision that they are taking, and all its implications.

Good decision-making requires a balance between efficiency and enabling the board to get to the heart of the matter, understanding the education world but bringing the outside world in, considering the current trends and what might have impact and what might get in the way. Some decisions cannot be rushed, while other matters are simply not important enough to warrant a long conversation.

Making a good decision involves consideration of a range of factors:

- based on the underpinning values
- funding pressures and incentives
- professional advice, based on leaders' experience and the evidence base
- parent/pupil voice
- knowledge of the school's context
- an assessment of what the staff will manage or support
- what's best for all children, including in other schools in the locality, while ensuring disadvantaged children and those with SEND get a fair deal

The balance between offering leadership and maintaining impartiality is one of the most difficult tasks required of the chair. Other governors and the head rely on the impartiality of the chair. If the governing board is to discuss an item on which the chair has strong views, it is good practice for the chair to ask the vice chair to chair for that item; in this way the chair can speak freely, but without as much influence on the process for arriving at a decision.

It is up to the chair to try to prevent tensions between individuals becoming a conflict and not to contribute to them inadvertently; to protect those who express a minority view; to see to it that no governor feels intimidated by the headteacher or by another governor; and to ensure that all governors respect the rights and responsibilities of the headteacher.

Although it is important that the chair remains as emotionally uninvolved as possible, chairing a board involves much more than tending to the rational and dispassionate dispatch of business. It is also about recognising the board as a human beings with group dynamics that can affect its ability to function well. The chair needs to reflect on any emotions s/he is experiencing and those being displayed by other trustees. The chair's role is to notice patterns of behaviour and help board colleagues work productively together.

Many governing boards rarely hold formal votes on issues, except the necessary shows of hands for agreement to, for example, accept a specific recommendation that needs to be properly proposed, agreed and minuted. Some feel that if a governing board is trying to resolve an issue through voting, this may be a sign of:

- a very divisive or complex issue, which might benefit from deferment for one meeting and further investigation or consultation
- a divided governing board where cliques have formed
- a very fundamental change which the board wants documented in this way

However, difference of opinion is an inevitable part of decision-making, and it is important that all feel able to register their opinion without that escalating into a conflict. Where concerns are apparent, these must be explored. Research shows that teams who do not always agree make better decisions and achieve more than teams who are always in agreement. Debate is healthy, and governors need to be able to challenge each other as well as the headteacher. When people become entrenched in their views, the chair has to manage the situation carefully so that relationships are not damaged and the group is not prevented from making a corporate decision.

Some chairs feel that having to resort to a vote is a failure on their part to win an argument or otherwise achieve a consensus, but it is a perfectly valid way of coming to a conclusion and can emphasise the responsibilities of the board for decisions. The chair needs to be seen as impartial, allowing adequate constructive deliberation and avoiding steamrollering. On occasion, it may be better to go to a vote to seek resolution and secure commitment to a corporate decision so that a damaging disagreement does not carry on.

The quorum for any governing board meeting or vote must be:

- In maintained schools: one half (rounded up to a whole number) of the complete membership of the governing body, excluding vacancies. For example, if the full membership is 12 and there is one vacancy, then the quorum for a governing body meeting is six governors (one half of 11 rounded up).
- In academies: three governors or trustees or one third of the governors or trustees in office (rounded up), whichever is greater. Some decisions require a different quorum. (The academy trust's own documentation should be consulted to confirm if there is any deviation from this common model.)

In the event of a tied vote, the chair may vote again with a casting vote. In setting the terms of reference for academy committees, the academy trust will consider whether to include provision for the chair to have a casting vote. In parliament, a casting vote is always used in favour of the status quo to keep things as they are. There is no such requirement of governing boards, but the chair should always think carefully before using the casting vote as s/he may want to come to a decision in another way, for example, at a later meeting, which would have additional information.

Governors should leave the meeting with the feeling that things have been achieved, that all members have been involved, that the occasion has been a worthwhile use of their time and skills and that some benefit will derive to the pupils in the school.

Following up decisions

Meeting minutes should clearly indicate action points, and to whom they have been allocated by the meeting. In conjunction with the clerk, the chair has a responsibility to chase progress between meetings to ensure that people are aware of what they undertook to do, and are doing it in the time frame agreed.

6.6 Chair's action between meetings

Governing boards are corporate bodies with collective responsibility; no governor may act in isolation, including the chair. However, the chair may take urgent action on behalf of the governing board when:

- it is not possible to call a governing board or committee meeting before the decision has to be made

- not to act would be seriously detrimental to the interests of the school, the pupils, their parents, or anyone employed at the school

An example of such action might be when immediate disciplinary action needs to be initiated against the headteacher. Regulations forbid the chair or the vice chair taking decisions on behalf of the governing board in relation to alterations to the school day; the closure of the school; changes of school category; approval of the budget; or on changes to policies relating to discipline and admissions. All actions taken by the chair alone should be reported to the governing board as soon as possible, and it is less likely to cause difficulties if the chair acts within boundaries set by clear governing board policies.

The school staff need to be aware of how and in what urgent circumstances the chair is to be contacted. Access to the chair must not become a way of undermining the headteacher. The chair's personal contact details must not be passed on to anyone without the chair's specific agreement, but there should be an address on the website through which the governing board can be contacted. This can be via the clerk.

In addition to these urgent tasks, the chair may also have to deal with correspondence on the governing board's behalf and this will need to be reported at the next meeting. The chair will usually also have a role in dealing with complaints, although NGA suggests this role could be reviewed as it can

be a drain on a chair's time without necessarily adding value to the process.

It is important that chairs are not drawn into making management decisions. The head will of course sometimes want to seek advice from the chair, but this is best done in their regular meetings (see chapter 4.1). Staff at the school should not get into the habit of telephoning the chair for a view on non-urgent matters and the chair should discourage this.

It is important that the chair gets to know the school and may visit for this purpose, but such visits should not become frequent, and need to follow the protocol for governors' visits; see Welcome to Governance.

 Checklist: leading the governing board business

- Are the papers the governing board receives timely in advance of meetings and fit for purpose?

- Have you reviewed the governance structures: are the committees the right ones?

- Is the balance of the work correct between the three core functions: strategy, monitoring and financial oversight?

- Has your governing board adopted a code of practice? If not, NGA has a model version you can adapt at www.nga.org.uk/Knowledge-Centre.

- Do you spend more than 30 days a year on school business? If yes, then you may be stepping over into the operational side. It would be worth seeking a mentor or a coach to review this.

- Does the vice chair share some of the chair's business?

- Does the clerk have a job description, and how is your clerk performance managed?

- Is your clerk accredited? If not, consider this route; for more details see www.nga.org.uk/clerking.

- Is your governing board able to carry out its financial duties well?

- Do you spend too much meeting time reviewing policies and checking compliance, rather than monitoring the impact on the children?

- Is the governing board delegating as much as it can to the headteacher and her/his staff?

Leaving the chair

7

The chair may resign at any time by giving notice in writing to the clerk. However, it is helpful under normal circumstances that notice is given and succession is planned.

A chair may serve to the end of her/his term of office, which will be anywhere from one year to four years at a time. NGA recommends one-year terms of office, as that makes it easier to review performance and hold an election. It is good practice for candidates to put themselves forward in advance, rather than at the meeting. This allows other governors to come forward for nomination, although many governors find this very hard to do when an existing chair signals her/his willingness to continue. However, this culture will need to change if we are to improve the current situation of too many long-serving chairs being at the helm as a school loses its way.

The school may want to introduce its own limit on the length of time an individual can chair at the same school or trust: NGA recommends six years. If everyone is clear that before six years are over the chair will step down, it requires the governing board to plan for a successor. The last act of a good chair is to ensure that the succession to the chair is planned and secure (see below).

DfE competencies for a chair: part 6

- understands the importance of succession planning to the ongoing effectiveness of both the board and the organisation

- recognises and develops talent in board members and ensures they are provided with opportunities to realise their potential

- develops the competence of the vice chair, including to act as chair should the need arise

- puts the needs of the board and organisation ahead of their own personal ambition and is willing to step down or move on at the appropriate time

7.1 Resigning

Chairs of schools in difficulty should consider resigning, in particular where it is absolutely clear that the governing board has not carried out its accountability role effectively. Where there has been fraud/embezzlement, or where the school has entered 'special measures', resignation should be the expected course of action, especially when the governing board was unaware of the problems.

NGA also recommends that no one serves as chair in one school for more than six years. Some long-standing chairs argue that they have to stay on as there is no one to take on the role. However, as developing the team is a core part of the chair's role, a good chair will have ensured this is not the case by planning for someone else to take her/his place. Many chairs have said they wish to serve more than six years. We suggest they volunteer for the governing board of another school, bringing their experience to this school, and in time may be able to serve as chair in that school. We appreciate that governors, particularly chairs, develop a bond with their school and a place in its community that will be missed, but there are other volunteering roles within a school if maintaining a connection is important.

As in all sectors, governance exists as a check on the power of an individual lead executive – in schools this is usually the headteacher. But undue executive influence must not be replaced by the undue influence of a chair or, more likely in practice, a working relationship between the head and the chair that excludes others and loses the benefit of their ideas and challenges. Ofsted has identified long service as one of the warning signs of a governing board that has stagnated. A healthy culture includes a mix of more experienced and newer members. If the school adopts NGA's recommended practice of chairs not serving more than six years, the risks of personality issues, cosiness with the head or unduly influential cliques developing are reduced.

> With effective succession planning in place, it can be beneficial for strong chairs to move on to another school or trust after a reasonable time (eg two terms of office). This can help to share expertise across the system and prevent boards stagnating or individuals gaining too much power and influence solely through their length of service.

DfE Governance Handbook, October 2020

7.2 Succession planning

All senior managers and leaders should give serious thought to matters of succession, ie identifying and developing individuals to equip them with the skills to step into a role when others step down. Yet in practice the stepping down of a governing board chair often results in a situation where an unprepared governor is pressed to stand for the post or a vacant position while a reluctant vice chair stands in. This must be avoided by the chair, who should lead the board in the process of devising a succession plan with all other governors engaged in discussions about the right person to take over. This might be from within the existing governing board or by recruiting new governors with the skills to become a chair at a later date.

The reasons sometimes given for not wanting to stand as chair reinforce the important role the current chair has in encouraging people to come forward:

- overwhelming demands of the job – the chair needs to show that it is manageable

- the time to do it – again, the chair needs to model good practice by demonstrating that the role can be performed effectively with a reasonable time commitment – hours not days per month on average (see chapter 2.4)

- not understanding the role – the current chair needs to ensure that all governors have a clear perspective of the role and not shroud their work in secrecy

- the chair does everything – delegate responsibilities and tasks for individual governors, working parties and committees to reinforce the perception that governance is a shared accountability not only vested in the chair

- governance experience and education knowledge – the experience of chairing can be gained in a wide range of roles and sectors, and years on the board is not necessarily a good indicator of suitability for chairing. Succession should be based on skill, capacity and willingness, not length of service.

- governors are not effectively prepared for the role – support and training for aspiring chairs should be provided ahead of election as well as once in post

- lack of confidence – some people lack the confidence to take on the role despite having the skills to chair, so their skills need to be recognised by the current chair and support offered, including a mentor

- governors hope someone else will volunteer – governors may well not see themselves as potential candidates so the chair may need to ask certain individuals to consider the possibility well before s/he steps down

- off-putting behaviours and attitude of the head or governing board – these issues are for the existing chair to deal with (see chapter 3.2) and attempt to leave an improved situation for a successor. Addressing issues of board dynamics will make the task of finding a successor easier

- existing chair is an impossible act to follow – the chair may welcome this reputation but it is not healthy for the school and that chair must make it clear that s/he is not indispensable

- perception that the role is for older people – age must not be seen as a barrier to taking the chair role and the current chair should consider the potential and capacity of all governors, not just those in more senior age brackets

A chair should try several tactics to ensure others will put themselves forward for election as chair:

- reviewing the role of the clerk, ensuring that arrangements allow for maximum support and advice, and demonstrating a positive working relationship with the clerk

- offering less daunting opportunities by encouraging other skilled governors to volunteer to be vice chair and chairs of committees and including them in some of the chair's activities, such as meetings with the headteacher

- develop the relationship with the vice chair and provide meaningful responsibilities that build confidence

- encouraging governors to go on leadership development training. NGA's Leading Governance programme, Development for Chairs, is available to all chairs, vice chairs and future chairs and is fully funded by the Department for Education (DfE). Please contact NGA for further information: leading.governance@nga.org.uk

- rotating the chairing of meetings to build experience of the role within the governing board

- indicating a personal limit to her/his term of office as chair, while offering to remain on the governing board to give support should the new chair welcome this

- if necessary, actively working with another governor to prepare her/him for the chair's role; s/he could spend a year as a shadow chair or even a co-chair

- should there be a deficit of volunteers from within existing governors despite all these attempts, the governing board needs to consider appointing a future chair to the next vacancy that arises

Developing a succession plan and identifying a future chair takes time and the right culture on the board to encourage governors to be honest about their intentions and aspirations for the future. Often this will only be possible in individual conversations with the chair, rather than full board meetings – an investment of time that will pay dividends in identifying future talent. Just as any recruitment activity has a cyclical nature, planning for succession will be more effective when it is reviewed regularly and scheduled into the annual work plan of meeting agendas to ensure that it does not become a reaction to a vacancy occurring in the chair position.

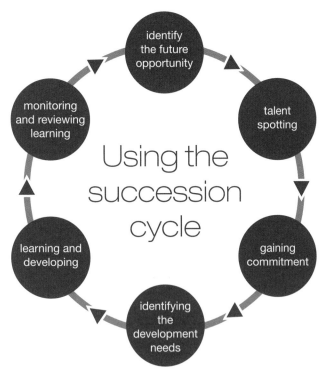

Using the succession cycle

- identify the future opportunity
- talent spotting
- gaining commitment
- identifying the development needs
- learning and developing
- monitoring and reviewing learning

Further information about developing a culture of succession and the succession cycle can be found in NGA's guidance "Preparing your board for the future", which can be downloaded from the NGA website www.nga.org.uk/Preparing-your-board-for-the-future.

> **“** The law does not prevent a board from advertising for a highly-skilled chair from outside the existing board where current governors or academy trustees do not wish to be appointed to the position. The successful candidate would need to be appointed to a vacant position on the board in accordance with the governing document. **”**
>
> DfE Governance Handbook, October 2020

Through our experience of leading a chairs recruitment service as part of Inspiring Governance, NGA established the concept of a future chair – a skilled volunteer who has the potential and the commitment to become a chair, vice chair or committee chair within a year of joining a school governing board. Volunteers who are experienced leaders, perhaps with a senior leadership role in their working life, charity trustee or other non-executive director experience are often undaunted by taking a chairing role soon after joining a new board, and have the capacity to absorb contextual knowledge about education and their setting quickly. In our experience, such candidates are open to the idea of discussing board leadership at the initial discussion or interview, and relish the challenge of chairing the board. Boards often recruit volunteers to strengthen certain areas of their board skills matrix, sometimes to fill a particular vacancy on a committee or a link role. Leadership should be viewed similarly as a skill that can be recruited to fill a gap in the board's leadership succession plan. The key is to be clear about the board's requirements in terms of skills and experience, including the timescale of succession to the chair, and not be afraid to broach the subject of chairing with suitable candidates.

7.3 Removing the chair mid-term

Any individual may lose the confidence of colleagues or become less effective in her/his role. There will be occasions when a governing board wishes to remove a serving chair from office before the end of her/his term. Clearly it would be desirable for governors to make their concerns felt to a chair informally before resorting to formal procedure at a governing board meeting. In some cases, especially if it is halfway through the school year, the pragmatic approach may be to suggest the chair let it be known that s/he will not be standing for re-election the following September. If the chair initially rejects this idea, it can be suggested that s/he undertakes a 360-degree review.

In maintained schools, a proposal to remove a chair must be a specified item on the agenda of a meeting of the governing board, and the agenda must be circulated at least seven days in advance of the meeting. The governor(s) proposing the removal of the chair should state their reasons for bringing the proposal, and the chair should have the right of reply. The chair then leaves the room and the remaining governors vote on the proposal.

Academies' articles of association set out the procedure for the removal of the chair, which in the model articles designed for converter schools is very similar to that for maintained schools. Each academy will need to refer to its own documents to check the process for removal. A particular issue is that some academy articles require 14 days' notice of a governing board meeting, rather than the seven for maintained schools.

If the vote for removal is carried, the governing board should fill the vacancy at its next meeting with the vice chair acting up in the meantime. Although the governing board could immediately elect a new chair at the meeting at which the chair is removed, this may not give all governors the time to reflect on whether to volunteer. All members of the governing board should feel that they have an equal opportunity to put their name forward for chair, and if a 'ready-made' candidate is introduced it could feel like a coup. The governing board may wish to set a date for an additional meeting in order to elect a new chair if the next scheduled meeting is many weeks away.

Who else can remove the chair?

In maintained schools only the governing body itself or, in very limited circumstances, the secretary of state can remove the chair of the governing body. A governing body cannot remove the chair if s/he has been appointed by the secretary of state under the powers granted by section 67 of the Education and Inspections Act 2006. A local authority has no power to remove the chair of a governing body. If a local authority has concerns about the governance of a school, the proper procedure is for the local authority to write to the governing body outlining its concern(s).

The local authority can remove delegated powers from the whole governing body of a maintained school in certain circumstances and, in the case where the local authority has serious concerns about governors, it can issue a warning notice and seek permission from the secretary of state to replace a governing board with an interim executive board. Both of these circumstances relate to the entire governing body rather the chair in isolation.

In academies, if the secretary of state has concerns about the academy s/he can issue (and publish) a pre-warning and warning notice. Depending on the funding agreement, the secretary of state may have various powers to intervene, but in all academy trusts, this will include the power to terminate the funding agreement, which would result in the school being moved to a different trust or closed.

There has been a well-publicised case in which the chief executive of a multi academy trust (MAT) used his status as a founding member to remove the chair of the trust board. Such a route should never have been included in the articles of association. It is important that the chief executive is not a member of the academy trust and the DfE now insists that new trusts do not have employees serving as trust members. Although some trusts were allowed to set up with this provision, we advise any trust with such articles to amend them to ensure this accountability loophole is closed, and from March 2021, members cannot be employees of the trust, nor occupy staff establishment roles on an unpaid voluntary basis.

Further resources

General

Department for Education (October 2020) The Governance Handbook. Available: www.gov.uk/government/ publications/ governance-handbook. This handbook sets out the core functions and legal duties of governing boards in academies and maintained schools.

Department for Education (2017) A Competency Framework for Governance. Available: https://www.gov. uk/government/publications/governance-handbook. The framework is designed to help governing boards assess what knowledge, skills and behaviour are needed to govern the school, or group of schools, most effectively.

Fishel, David (2003) Boards That Work: a guide for charity trustees. London: Directory of Social Change.

NGA (2019) Welcome to Governance. Birmingham: National Governance Association. Available: www.nga.org.uk/ publications.This NGA guide is a useful resource for chairs to issue to their new governors. GOLD members of NGA get a free copy when they register a new governor.

NGA (2019) Welcome to a Multi Academy Trust. Birmingham: National Governance Association. Available: www.nga.org. uk/publications. This guide provides high-quality practical information on MAT governance structure and practice for new trustees and senior leaders, whether or not they have previous experience of governing in standalone schools or organisations in other sectors. The third edition will be publish mid January 2019.

Ofsted (2011) School Governance: learning from the best. Available: https://www.gov.uk/government/uploads/system/ uploads/attachment_data/file/413583/School_governance_ learning_from_the_best.doc. Last accessed 20 September 2020.

There are also a range of resources available in NGA's Knowledge Centre: www.nga.org.uk/Knowledge-Centre

Chapter 1 – Leading governance in schools

APPG on Education Governance and Leadership (2015) 20 Questions for the Governing Boards to ask itself. Available: www.nga.org.uk/20questions. Last accessed 21 September 2020. www.nga.org.uk/twenty-questions

APPG on Education Governance and Leadership (2015) 21 Questions for Multi Academy Trusts. Available: www.nga. org.uk/21questions. Last accessed 21 September 2020.

The Ethical Leadership Commission included senior representatives across the education sector and its final report, Navigating the educational moral maze, was launched at a summit at the Institute of Education in London with the Framework for Ethical Leadership in Education in January 2019. www.nga.org.uk/ethicalleadership

Department for Education (2010) The Importance of Teaching: the schools white paper 2010. Available: https://www.gov.uk/ government/publications/the-importance-of-teaching-the-schools-white-paper-2010. Last accessed 21 September 2020.

Garratt, Bob (2010) The Fish Rots From The Head: developing effective board directors. London: Profile Books.

James, C et al (2012) The Chair of the Board: a review of the literature. CfBT.

James, C et al (2013) The Chair of the School Governing Board in England: roles, relationships, and responsibilities. CfBT.

Myners, P (2014) Report of the Independent Governance Review. Available: https://www.co-operative.coop/investors/ myners-report. Last accessed 21 September 2020.

NGA has published a series called Taking the Next Steps alongside the Association of School and College Leaders and Browne Jacobson. Available: http://www.nga.org.uk/taking-the-next-step. Last accessed 20 September 2020. This joint guidance takes the form of three papers designed to help school leaders, trustees and governors to better understand the current policy landscape, consider their options and make the best long-term decisions for their school.

Chapter 2 – Becoming the chair

National Leaders of Governance: (NLGs) are chairs of governors who have been designated by the DfE and are available to support chairs in other schools, whether a new chair of governors, or chairs who are experiencing particular challenges. There is no charge for NLG time, which is largely mentoring or coaching. However, some NLGs also offer training or governance reviews for which they will usually charge. A list of NLGs is available at http://apps.nationalcollege.org.uk/s2ssd_new/. Alternatively email governors.mailbox@education.gov.uk

National Leaders of Governance Advisory Group (September 2020) DfE Ministers invited school governance sector leaders, and experienced governors and school leaders to form an external advisory group, which was commissioned to make recommendations for improvements to the current NLG programme. This report presents the advisory group's recommendations for a reformed NLG programme. https://assets.publishing.service.gov.uk/government/uploads/system/uploads/attachment_data/file/916114/NLG_Reform-Advisory_Group_Report_Sep_2020.pdf

NGA (2016) Time to Chair – how chairs spend their time. Available: www.nga.org.uk/timetochair. Last accessed 21 September 2020

NGA (2020) Time to chair? Exploring the time commitments of chairs of multi academy trusts (MATs) www.nga.org.uk/timetochairaMAT.

Chapter 3 – Leading and developing the team

The Inspiring Governance service commenced in September 2016 and is a free online recruitment service funded by the Department for Education connecting skilled volunteers with recruiting boards until at least March 2021. See www.inspiringgovernance.org for more information.

Inspiring Governance Partnership (2020) Right People Around the Table. Available: www.nga.org.uk/rightpeoplearoundthetable. Last accessed 20 September 2020. A practical guide designed to help school governors and trustees plan and carry out recruitment and induction. The guide highlights good practice for induction, training and succession.

NGA (2020) Model Code of Conduct. Available: www.nga.org.uk/codeofconduct. Last accessed 20 September 2020.

NGA (2020) Skills Audit and Matrix. Available: www.nga.org.uk/skills-audit. Last accessed 20 September 2020. NGA has produced two separate audits; one for those governing a single school and one for those governing a group of schools.

Leading Governance
NGA delivers Leading Governance programmes across England. You can access at least £1,000 of DfE funding to support your governing board's development through NGA's (currently remote-delivery) Leading Governance programmes. Programmes include development for chairs, clerks, and boards, and provide opportunities to develop skills and confident governance. www.nga.org.uk/leadinggovernance

Chapter 4 – The chair, the headteacher and accountability

Otto, S (2003) Not So Very Different: a comparison of the roles of chairs of governing bodies and managers in different sectors. Cornforth, C. (2005) The Governance of Public and Non-Profit Organisations: what do board chairs do? London: Routledge.

NGA, ASCL,LGA, NAHT and ISBL (2019) What governing boards and school leaders should expect from each other. Available: www.nga.org.uk/what-we-expect. Last accessed 20 September 2020.

NGA, DfE (2017) A Guide to Recruiting and Selecting a New Headteacher. Available: www.nga.org.uk/recruitingguidance. Last accessed 20 September 2020.

NGA, NFER, TFLT (2016) Executive Headteachers: what's in a name? Available: www.nga.org.uk/whats-in-a-name. Last accessed 20 September 2020.

Buck, A (2018) Leadership Matters 3.0: How leaders at all levels can create great schools. John Catt Educational Ltd; Third, UPDATED AND REVISED Edition (8 Aug. 2018)

NFER (2017) Keeping Your Head: NFER analysis of headteacher retention. Available: https://www.nfer.ac.uk/publications/LFSC01/LFSC01.pdf. Last accessed 20 September 2020.

Chapter 5 – Leading school improvement

Ofsted (2019) School Inspection Handbook. Available: https://www.gov.uk/government/publications/school-inspection-handbook-eif. Last accessed 20 September 2020.

NGA et al (2015) Knowing Your School (briefing notes 1–6). Available: http://www.nga.org.uk/knowingyourschool. Last accessed 20 September 2020.

Chapter 6 – Leading governing board business

NGA, ASCL and NAHT (2020) Being Strategic: a guide for governing boards and school leaders. Available: www.nga.org.uk/BeingStrategic. Last accessed 9 October 2020.

Chapter 7 – Leaving the chair

NGA (2018) Right People Around The Table – succession planning: moving on and ensuring leadership. Last accessed 20 September 2020.

Inspiring Governance Future Chairs recruitment service: www.inspiringgovernance.org/volunteers/future-chairs-recruitment-service/